MARKETING TIPS

FOR

TRANSLATORS

The ultimate collection of tips
from the podcast

Tess Whitty

tess@marketingtipsfortranslators.com

Tess uses simple but powerful language to explain her experience and other translators' experience, so that anyone understands and, most importantly, implements her tips. She provides information about what to do, but also how to do it, without forgetting why we are supposed to do it. The best about this book is that it can be used equally by newcomers and by experienced translators in very different stages of their careers, as it is focused in different marketing strategies depending on one's needs. This is a must read for translators wanting to boost in their careers. - Margarita Arizmendi

If I were to choose a single word to describe Tess Whitty's latest book I would opt for "comprehensive". I used the word "comprehensive" because it goes beyond covering, for example, how to write a good CV and how to avoid CVs scams, or how to calculate your rates, to also cover how to avoid procrastination and implement an effective time management strategy, how to juggle work and personal life and so on. I would definitely recommend this book if you are a freelance translator wanting to make the most out of every single day of your professional life. – Francesca Calabrò

The book is full of excellent advice from Tess and other experienced translators. Whether you are a newbie or are a seasoned professional, you'll certainly find a piece of advice to help you further develop your business. I found the 'Getting clients' chapter extremely useful. Remembering that 'you are in charge' of the relationship with clients is essential. It takes a lot of courage (especially if you were previously an employee) to set yourself up as an equal, but many good things can come out of it. I would highly recommend the book to any language professionals looking for guidance and/or to spruce up their career. – Ramona Amuza

Tess Whitty's new book compiles conversations she has had with colleagues all over the world as part of her "Marketing Tips for Translators" podcast. It is more than interviews, each section in the seven chapters feels like a conversation, as if she, her guest and the reader were sitting in a cozy living room, perhaps by the fire and with a cup of hot chocolate, chatting about this delightful profession we share. Having read the Marketing Cookbook for Translators, I thought I knew all I needed, but this new book has plenty of new information, and reinforces some lessons from the past. Looking forward to the next one! – Christian Nielsen-Palacios

1

"Marketing tips for translators" discusses all the issues freelance translators need to think about from starting a translation business and finding clients to maintaining your skills and preparing for the future. It is well-organized and divided into topics, making specific information easy to find. Tess Whitty and her guests clearly know what they are talking about. *"Marketing tips for translators"* should be considered essential reading whatever stage you are at. — Louise Souter

Whitty nor Swedish Translation Services or any of the contributors are responsible for the success or failure of your business decisions.

Although the author and publisher have made every effort to ensure that the information in this book was correct at press time, the author and publisher do not assume and hereby disclaim any liability to any party for any loss, damage, or disruption caused by errors or omissions, whether such errors or omissions result from negligence, accident, or any other cause.

Translators are well equipped to thrive in an environment where education, hard work and attention to detail can yield large benefits. Among these benefits are the freedom to choose when to work, a steady income, and continual exposure to new people and stimulating ideas.

Effective marketing – of yourself, of your business – can help you reach the next level of success. The ideas and tools explored in this book have produced positive results for translators at every stage in the game and they will for you too, whether you are a translator who:

- Is just getting started as a freelance translator or interpreter,
- Needs proven marketing tactics and step-by-step strategies to create a steady stream of income, or
- Wants to take a translation career to the next level using marketing techniques and strategies.

If you find yourself in one of the above categories, hungry for the skills and tools that will grow your business – then this book can help.

Each section of this book is adapted from a podcast interview with an established translator or other professional. I started my website and podcast Marketing Tips for Translators [www.marketingtipsfortranslators.com/archive/podcast/] to connect with and share information within the international translation community. We have many issues and concerns in common and the podcast is a meeting ground of sorts for those of us who spend a lot of time alone working on documents.

The chapters in this book will help you discover the inspiration you need to market your translation services in an efficient way, as well as fresh ideas about productivity and tools for organizing your time and workday. We'll also cover proven methods and systems for marketing to your ideal potential clients, and strategies for maintaining a continuous marketing plan for finding new clients, keeping your existing clients, and getting the word out about your translation services. We'll show you how to get clients to find you, instead of you trying to find them.

The language will be more familiar or relaxed, since it is based on audio recordings. However, the tips are just as valuable, and are presented in a distilled, written format.

A SPECIAL THANKS

The Marketing Tips for Translators podcast would not exist without the contributions from all the people I interviewed during the first two years of the podcast. I extend my sincere thanks to all podcast interviewees. Not all could be featured in this book, and I have selected the content based on topics that have been especially popular among the episodes. I encourage you to go back to the podcast and look for other interviews and topics as well. There might be something just for you, which did not make it into this book [www.marketingtipsfortranslators.com/archive/podcast/]. I especially want to thank the people whose interviews have been the basis of the chapters in this book. Each contributor is mentioned at the end of each section, plus in the resources, with a link to their websites. Do check them out! Finally, I would like to thank my husband, who is always encouraging me in my entrepreneurial endeavors, and who many times has to "just do a quick read through" of my productions. Thank you also to my children, who both have helped with editing the podcast during different periods of the journey.

TABLE OF CONTENTS

EARLY REVIEWS... 1

LEGAL DISCLAIMER 3

INTRODUCTION.. 5

    HOW TO USE THIS BOOK.. 6

    A SPECIAL THANKS 7

CHAPTER 1 – GETTING STARTED 16

TRIAL AND ERROR – JUST GET STARTED 17

    GETTING EXPERIENCE 17

    TIPS FOR STARTING TO MARKET YOUR TRANSLATION SERVICES 18

    THE BIGGEST MISTAKES BEGINNERS MAKE 19

MASTERING LANGUAGE LEARNING FOR TRANSLATORS 20

    TRANSLATION AS A TOOL TO LEARN A LANGUAGE 20

        BOOKS.. 21

        SKYPE 21

        IMMERSION 21

HOW TO SPECIALIZE... 22

    THE BENEFITS OF SPECIALIZING 22

    WORK WITH A SPECIALIST 23

    TAKE UNIVERSITY LEVEL COURSES 23

WRITING CVS AND ALTERNATIVES TO CVS 24

    ADAPT YOUR CV 24

    MAKE USE OF DIGITAL FEATURES 25

    BE SPECIFIC.. 25

    AVOID THESE MISTAKES.. 25

    ALTERNATIVES TO CVs 26

CV SCAMS AND HOW TO AVOID THEM 27

    HOW DO PEOPLE USE FALSE CVs? 27

    WHAT CAN WE DO TO PREVENT PEOPLE FROM STEALING OUR
    INFORMATION AND PRETENDING TO BE US? 27

HOW TO CALCULATE YOUR RATES 29

    ESTABLISHING EARNING GOALS 29

    QUOTING 29

    CALCULATING RATES 30

INVOICING AND GETTING PAID 31

    BASIC INVOICING TIPS 31

    OVERDUE INVOICES 32

    MISTAKES THAT CAN LEAD TO YOU NOT GETTING PAID 33

WORKING WITH AGENCIES.. 34

    WHERE TO FIND THE GOOD AGENCIES 34

    HOW TO CONTACT THEM 34

    HOW CAN WE HELP AGENCIES FIND US? 35

    TEST TRANSLATIONS 36

    SIGNING CONTRACTS 36

    CREATING A FAVORABLE IMPRESSION 36

WHAT DO AGENCIES LOOK FOR IN FREELANCE TRANSLATORS? 38

    HOW DO AGENCIES DEAL WITH FALSE APPLICATIONS?........... 38

    WHAT NOT TO DO WHEN CONTACTING A TRANSLATION COMPANY 39

    WHAT TO DO WHEN CONTACTING A TRANSLATION COMPANY 39

CHAPTER 2 – GETTING CLIENTS.. 41

HOW TO MAKE YOUR TRANSLATION BUSINESS STAND OUT 42

    YOU ARE IN CHARGE 42

    AGENCIES, DIRECT CLIENTS, OR BOTH 43

    LOOKING AT OUR ATTITUDE.. 43

ATTITUDE AND CLIENTS 44

HOW TO POSITION OURSELVES AS EXPERTS 45

EFFECTIVE COMMUNICATION SKILLS FOR TRANSLATORS 46

TURNAROUND TIME 46

OTHER NEEDS CUSTOMERS MAY HAVE 47

THE VALUES YOU OFFER 47

IMPROVE COMMUNICATION – WRITTEN AND ORAL 48

TIPS FROM CJ HAYDEN'S GET CLIENTS NOW PROGRAM 51

MARKETING PIPELINE 52

SUCCESS INGREDIENTS 52

CHOOSING MARKETING ACTIVITIES 53

SUCCESS FACTORS FOR THE MARKETING PIPELINE 54

FOLLOWING UP 55

FACE-TO-FACE NETWORKING 56

HOW TO NETWORK 56

GET OVER THE FEAR 57

WHAT NETWORKS TO FOCUS ON 57

FOCUS ON HELPING 58

BEFORE THE EVENT 58

DURING THE EVENT 59

FOLLOW-UP 60

PRICING STRATEGIES 62

PRICING ZONES 62

EXTRA CHARGES AND DISCOUNTS 63

BY THE WORD, HOUR OR PROJECT? 64

PACKAGE PRICING 65

NEGOTIATING YOUR PRICES 66

RAISING YOUR RATES 67

VALUE PRICING 68

    HOW TO EARN MORE WITH EXISTING CLIENTS.. 69

HOW TO GET YOUR FIRST THREE DIRECT CLIENTS 70

    THREE ACTION STEPS TO REACH THESE FIRST DIRECT CLIENTS 70

    TIPS FOR REACHING THE LARGE NUMBERS.. 70

    USING OTHER SERVICE PROVIDERS 71

    LEVERAGING EXISTING RESOURCES AND CONTACTS 72

NEGOTIATION SKILLS 73

    HOW TO DEAL WITH DIFFICULT OR DEMANDING CLIENTS 74

    NEGOTIATION MISTAKES TO AVOID 75

UNDERSTANDING THE SALES PROCESS 77

    FIRST CONTACT 77

    MONITORING... 77

    CLOSING... 78

    BECOMING BETTER AT SELLING.. 79

CHAPTER 3 – MARKETING... 80

BRANDING FOR FREELANCERS 81

    HOW TO START BRANDING 81

    MISTAKES TO AVOID IN BRANDING.. 82

BUSINESS-TO-BUSINESS MARKETING 83

    HOW TO REACH OTHER BUSINESSES WITH OUR MARKETING MESSAGE 83

    THE FIVE MOST IMPORTANT TIPS WHEN MARKETING TO BUSINESSES... 84

HOW TO MARKET YOUR TRANSLATION SERVICES TO DIRECT CLIENTS YOU CANNOT MEET.. 85

    WARM EMAIL PROSPECTING.. 85

    STEALTH MARKETING 86

    MISTAKES WHEN MARKETING TO DIRECT CLIENTS................................. 86

ELEMENTS OF A MARKETING PLAN FOR TRANSLATORS 87

ANALYSIS 87

OBJECTIVES 88

PRODUCTS AND SERVICES OFFERED 90

BUDGET 90

MARKETING MATERIALS 91

CREATING "MARKETING PERSONAS" FOR YOUR FREELANCE TRANSLATION BUSINESS 93

USING MARKETING PERSONAS FOR IMPROVED MARKETING 94

QUESTIONS TO ASK WHEN DEVELOPING MARKETING PERSONAS 94

WARM EMAIL PROSPECTING FOR TRANSLATORS 96

THE DIFFERENCE FROM SENDING A REGULAR SALES LETTER OR EMAIL.. 97

PAY ATTENTION TO THE SUBJECT LINE 97

DOING THE RESEARCH 98

END WITH A CALL TO ACTION 100

LEAD NURTURING 100

MARKETING FOR LITERARY TRANSLATORS 101

START WITH CONTACTING SMALLER PUBLISHERS 101

AND AUTHORS 101

CREATE A PORTFOLIO 102

CHAPTER 4 – PRODUCTIVITY 103

TIME MANAGEMENT AND FINDING BALANCE 104

JUGGLING WORK AND LIFE 104

BIGGEST CHALLENGES WITH TIME MANAGEMENT 105

DISTRACTIONS 106

TACKLING PROCRASTINATION 107

WORKSPACE 108

HOW TO GET THINGS DONE 109

FIND A PROCRASTINATION BUDDY 109

DAILY ACTION PACKS 111

CREATING FOCUS 112

ORGANIZING YOUR BRAIN 112

WORKING EFFICIENTLY AND PREPARING FOR TIME OFF 115

TRACK YOUR TIME 115

TO-DO LISTS 116

GET ORGANIZED 116

PRIORITIZE TASKS TO GET THEM DONE 117

FOCUS 117

END YOUR WORKDAY 118

STRESS-RELEASE 118

TAKE THE VACATION 120

HOW TO GET RID OF DIGITAL CLUTTER 122

DECLUTTERING EMAIL 122

FILE MANAGEMENT 122

ORGANIZING PASSWORDS 123

PROCRASTINATION AND TACKLING BIGGER PROJECTS 123

THE FEAST OR FAMINE CYCLE 124

CHAPTER 5 – TOOLS 125

HOW TO ORGANIZE AND KEEP A PAPERLESS OFFICE 126

KEEPING DIGITAL DOCUMENTS SAFE 126

TOOLS 127

PRODUCTIVITY AND ORGANIZATION APPS FOR TRANSLATORS 128

GETTING TO INBOX ZERO 130

SEPARATE INBOXES 131

ACTIONABLE OR NOT? 131

FILTERS 132

HOW TO USE A WEBSITE TO MARKET YOUR TRANSLATION SERVICES 133

PLANNING THE WEBSITE 133

CONTENT 134

DESIGN 135

SEARCH ENGINE MARKETING 136

MARKETING AND PROMOTING YOUR WEBSITE 138

MORE TIPS TO PROMOTE YOUR WEBSITE OFFLINE 139

PROVIDING PROOF OF YOUR SKILLS 140

USING INFORMATION PRODUCTS TO ADD VALUE TO YOUR WEBSITE 141

HOW TO PROVIDE MORE VALUE TO A WEBSITE 142

A TYPICAL SALES CYCLE FOR POTENTIAL CLIENTS THAT FIND YOUR
WEBSITE 143

BUILDING TRUST 143

SEO TIPS FOR TRANSLATORS 144

KEYWORDS 144

NEW RULES ABOUT OPTIMIZATION FOR GOOGLE 145

BLOGGING FOR TRANSLATORS 146

BLOGGING FOR CLIENTS 146

HOW TO START A BLOG 146

USING LINKEDIN TO MARKET TRANSLATION SERVICES 148

PROFILE 148

COMMON MISTAKES 149

GROUPS 149

USING THE SEARCH FUNCTION 149

CONNECTING 150

GOOGLE+ TIPS FOR TRANSLATORS 151

SEO 151

CONTENT-CENTRIC 152

GOOGLE+ PAGE 152

GOOGLE+ GROUPS.. 152

GOOGLE+ PROFILE VERSUS PAGE 153

GOOGLE ADS AS A MARKETING TOOL FOR TRANSLATORS 154

HOW TO GET STARTED 155

MONITORING THE CAMPAIGN 156

SETUP 156

TWEAKING FOR RESULTS 157

CHAPTER 6 – INTO THE FUTURE... 159

HOW TO BECOME A WORLD-CLASS TRANSLATOR 160

HUMILITY 160

COLLABORATION 160

PERSEVERANCE 161

HAVING A CONTINUING EDUCATION STRATEGY............................ 163

MAINTAINING YOUR SECOND LANGUAGE 164

PROTECTING YOURSELF AND YOUR BUSINESS................................ 165

HOW DO WE PROTECT OUR BUSINESS ASSETS? 165

HOW DO WE PROTECT AND CULTIVATE OUR MOTIVATION AND
BALANCE? 167

HAVING A WORKING STRATEGY FOR YOUR BUSINESS 168

CONCLUSION 170

CHAPTER 7 – CONTRIBUTORS 171

LIST OF CONTRIBUTORS TO THIS BOOK...................................... 171

FURTHER READING 174

CHAPTER 1 – GETTING STARTED

First steps in any profession are always a bit scary, and setting up shop as a freelance translator is no different. I consulted a wide range of experts on the subject of getting started, and their most popular tip is to just dive right in. This tip is closely followed by learning to set the right price for your services. For this chapter, I've collected established international translators' practical advice for beginners and mid-career translators seeking to grow their freelance business (gleaned from my podcast Marketing Tips for Translators – find out more about these translation professionals at the end of each section.

TRIAL AND ERROR – JUST GET STARTED

You learn how to run a freelance business through trial and error, mostly error. Freelancing can be a real struggle for many people. How do you invoice a client for the first time, how much do you charge, how do you find your second and third clients? For freelancers, the most important strategy or step is to just do it; just get started.

GETTING EXPERIENCE

No client wants to hire someone with zero experience; however, in translation it is a little easier to gain some than in other professions. For example, you can get a part-time position at an agency, even if it's just as a trainee, to get experience and see how things work, to learn about things like quality assurance, how to build a clientele, etc. You could also volunteer with organizations such as Translators without Borders. Here you would complete a screening test and someone would check the quality of your work. If you are accepted, you would have the opportunity to participate in several projects, which you could then highlight and use as experience on your CV. You could also offer pro bono services to other nongovernmental organizations to get valuable experience.

TIPS FOR STARTING TO MARKET YOUR TRANSLATION SERVICES

- Do a little bit every day. A lot of us think about that big block of time when we are going to accomplish a large objective or complete a major project. But, unless you don't need to work to support yourself, and have no responsibilities to other people, that big block of time is never coming.

- Don't expect too much return for too little effort. I talk to a lot of beginning translators who say they are discouraged because they have sent out 25 resumes and don't have any work yet. It takes about a year to start making real money, so don't expect too much for too little. Try a variety of strategies. Don't depend too heavily on any one approach.

- Build a website – it can cost almost nothing if you have even minimal web design skills. Or use a free service such as WordPress and just pay for your domain name and web hosting. Or, you can have someone create your website. You really only need one page highlighting who you are, a second outlining the services you provide, and a third page for contact information. If you create a site through WordPress, you will always have the opportunity to make changes yourself, without involving web developers. If you do decide to pay someone, include that cost from the outset, when you are building your business plan.

- Apply to good agencies. Pre-qualify for your chosen agencies through Payment Practices [www.paymentpractices.net/], or the ProZ.com Blue Board [www.proz.com/blueboard], or other professional organizations. Join a translator association such as International Association of Professional Translators and Interpreters (IAPTI) [www.iapti.org/]. Association directories can be a valuable resource for finding clients and for having clients find you.

You must take the long view so you don't end up stuck forever in the low-paying market. And you may need to either get another job, or dip into some significant savings, or decrease your living expenses to the point where you can live on what you are making as a translator. People can panic when it comes to money. They take whatever work comes in the door and get stuck in that low-paying market. Then they have no time to acquire higher-paying clients because they must work so many hours to make a living.

From interview with **Corinne McKay** *[www.thoughtsontranslation.com], a certified French to English translator, author and educator.*

Learning a language is not a linear process; it's a progression that builds upon prior knowledge. You must create a foundation for the language, and it's not about the way you use learning materials; it's about the way you absorb them. It's not a matter of learning anything by heart; it's a matter of learning the basic structure and syntax of language (how you put sentences together) and its intonation. One approach is to refrain from learning single words to form sentences, but to instead be exposed to whole sentences, and then go deeper to figure out how each single component is supposed to be pronounced. It is the opposite of what people normally do in school.

There is no definitive way to learn a language; there is no best method. It just comes down to what you like doing. At the same time, this method can work for a lot of people – they try it and it works.

TRANSLATION AS A TOOL TO LEARN A LANGUAGE

A lot of theories out there state, for example, that you should avoid using your mother tongue because we tend to filter everything through our own native language. But translation is an amazing tool to figure out the patterns in another language simply by comparing. Let's say you are a native Swedish speaker and you are learning English, or you are learning German; you could infer a lot of the rules without needing grammatical explanations – just by comparing two texts. So imagine that when you start to learn a language, instead of taking boring classes, you just take some learning materials that have one language on one page and the other language on the other page and compare the two languages. You learn the rules of how grammar and syntax work simply through comparison.

If you think about it, kids don't learn words by hearing a single word; they extract single words from a flow of words because they hear their parents using full sentences. That's how we should learn. Learning a language the natural way is much easier than people think.

BOOKS

One of the finest book series for learning languages is called Assimil. The title comes from the word assimilate. It is probably the best, or at least the most popular, language theory series in Europe. While it's surprisingly not as well-known in the United States, it is one of the best in the world. The books are small and portable enough to carry around with you.

SKYPE

You can literally learn a language by talking to people on Skype. What is special about this approach is that you are going to develop language skills simply by talking about things you like. You can talk about any complex subject in very simple terms and it works, especially in combination with using learning materials.

IMMERSION

Language learning is not about being bent over books; it is about getting out there, getting familiar with people, and being proactive. Language learning is about living. A lot of problems arise when people see languages as subjects to study in school instead of tools that we could use to improve our lives.

From Interview with Luca Lampariello [*www.thepolyglotdream.com*], *a translator and language teacher.*

HOW TO SPECIALIZE

Most of us have taken on a translation project and soon realized that we should not have taken it on. It happens from time to time; you just don't have the same sense of confidence in those projects that you do for those in your core area. So how do you get that confidence?

THE BENEFITS OF SPECIALIZING

Increased credibility, respect, productivity and income! All of these are great reasons to specialize. When you can mingle in a roomful of potential customers and talk about their subject as a peer, when you know the answer to 90% of the term queries translation colleagues ask in your field off the top of your head, you can call yourself a specialist. We all know it when we see it. The more you specialize, the faster you work. You have less background research to do, because you know the subject well. Marketing may pay off faster when you're only targeting a narrow area. There's also that intangible satisfying feeling that you got it right, and knowing that the text you delivered is excellent.

There is a downside though: you must say no a lot. You will be offered projects that are not in the field that you are targeting and you will have to learn to refuse that work if you truly want to focus on your core area of expertise. Adding a referral to a trusted colleague who does work in that field is a great way to sweeten the "No".

WORK WITH A SPECIALIST

Working with a specialist is usually the best method. Often a translator becomes a specialist because they have had a prior career in an industry or have an in-house helper for terminology, e.g., a medical translator whose partner is a nurse or doctor. If you can work with a friend or family member who is a specialist in a particular field, you will learn and grow your subject matter expertise with every job. Alternatively, you could work with a translator who is already a specialist in that area; for example, if you want to be an oil and gas specialist, offer to read oil and gas specialist translators' work. Study how they do it. Obviously, if you can get paid for editing, or paid for translations, or have your own translations proofread by someone else while you learn and grow, that's even better.

TAKE UNIVERSITY LEVEL COURSES

Many excellent opportunities exist for learning about whatever subject you might want to specialize in these days. The limits are discipline, enthusiasm and time, since now much quality material is free and readily available online. Coursera and other massive open online course platforms provide a wealth of high quality material. See what you can find, and dive in!

*From interview with **Karen Tkaczyk** [www.mcmillantranslation.com], a PhD chemist, French into English technical translator, and an editor specializing in chemistry.*

Many translation companies have expressed concerns about some of the CVs they receive from potential translators. They can be badly written, or exclude important information, or even have spelling errors. Other companies are not interested in receiving CVs at all.

It's essential to decide whether a CV or a resume is the right document to send to a particular client. Many, especially direct clients, don't want to look at CVs; they prefer to operate on a business-to-business level. They are more interested in what you are offering than in your background. So, if you want to use your CV to market your services, you need to understand in which settings and situations a CV will work best. Here are a few tips:

ADAPT YOUR CV

We are translators, and we usually have a specialization or area of expertise – our CVs need to reflect this. If we send our CV to a company that is looking for people for a particular project and they have a set of expectations regarding their ideal translator, we can be successful only if we seem relevant to what they are expecting.

The solution is to have different versions of your CV. Each of them should relate to what you do and who you are, but they should each present your experience and background knowledge in a slightly different way. Have one that concentrates on legal translation, or one that is related to marketing and business, one that is slightly skewed towards interpreting, and so on. Maintain different versions and make sure you send the most appropriate version for each request that you receive.

MAKE USE OF DIGITAL FEATURES

We live in a digital age. Hardly anyone prints CVs on paper anymore. It's much more likely that somebody at an agency will receive a CV as a PDF document and look at it on the computer screen. It is so easy to add a couple of hyperlinks here and there (a link to a LinkedIn profile, for example, or maybe a link to samples of your translations) that anyone can click on directly from the document. For interpreters, imagine the difference between a normal CV and a CV that contains a link to a sample of your voice. You can be sure that somebody is going to click on the latter. Be imaginative. For example, you could record a sales pitch about why they should pick you as an interpreter and embed it directly in your CV.

BE SPECIFIC

The way in which we present information is important. We need to be as specific as possible about our experience and try to qualify it. So, rather than saying you have vast experience in a certain area, try to give very specific details about that experience. The more specific we are, the more credible we will seem to the people who read our CVs.

AVOID THESE MISTAKES

Avoid sending a CV when another document might be more appropriate. Many direct clients and company owners don't want to see a CV; they would prefer to see a business profile, a brochure, or a detailed offer. When I talk to people who have their own businesses they may say, for example, that if they are looking for a graphic designer, they want to see portfolios; they want to see what the designer can do. It is the same thing when they are looking for a copywriter or a translator. A CV won't necessarily tell them what they need to know about you.

25

Think twice about using an employment format for your CV. As a freelancer, you have you own business, so don't list the positions you've held or give your education precedence over your experience, as you would if you were looking for a job.

ALTERNATIVES TO CVS

Consider alternatives to CVs such as brochures. A marketing brochure is a document that outlines everything you do, with a brief introduction to the services you offer and a description of your values on the first page. On the following three pages, describe the services you provide in detail, giving examples of the type of document you most often translate. You can use this brochure to educate both existing and potential clients by including a list of the benefits for clients who use your services. Include a call to action on each page asking them to get in touch so you may discuss their project.

Another alternative to consider is a business profile – something halfway between a CV and a website. It could be a longer PDF document that outlines your experience and your background, as well as explaining why that should matter to your client. So rather than describing what a diploma in translation is, give them a list of the benefits they would be getting by hiring a translator that has one.

From interview with Marta Stelmaszak
[www.wantwords.co.uk/martastelmaszak], a communication specialist who specializes in English to Polish translation with a focus on business and economics.

CV SCAMS AND HOW TO AVOID THEM

Many freelancers have been subject to CV scams. A CV scam is when someone gets hold of your CV, replaces the personal information and a few other details, and uses it as their own.

HOW DO PEOPLE USE FALSE CVS?

Some people send fake emails to translation agencies claiming to be a particular translator. They must hope that the agency will be desperate for a translator in the exact combinations that they claim to have. They generally use Google Translate to make a translation and hope to get at least a minimum fee for it. They don't do free test translations, only translations that are paid.

Another common scam involves downloading translators' online CVs or work histories and personalizing them to appear as the scammer's own.

WHAT CAN WE DO TO PREVENT PEOPLE FROM STEALING OUR INFORMATION AND PRETENDING TO BE US?

- Remove your CV from the Internet. Remember that there may be cached versions of it. When someone you trust asks you for a CV, send them a password protected PDF instead. Do not use Word or any kind of text editor to create a finished document that will circulate.

- Ask people to connect with you on LinkedIn. There they can have a look at your profile and see what you've been doing. Of course, this depends on how specialized you are. You may also ask the person that wants your CV to take a look at your LinkedIn profile first, and then you send a short reference list of relevant assignments for this particular customer.

27

- You can always get your own domain name if you don't have one already, and stop using free services like Hotmail and Gmail. For very little money (20 USD or EUR per year) you can get your own domain name and ensure that you receive all your translation-related emails there.

- If you do send out a CV, make sure you know to whom you are sending it by researching that person. Ensure that they have a physical address and that you have accurate contact information.

- Use privacy settings, not just for LinkedIn, but for every kind of portal you use. Make sure that your information isn't public, and make it visible only to your contacts on that portal.

From interview with Irene Elmerot
[www.translationcorner.se/team/irene-elmerot], a Swedish freelance translator and proofreader.

HOW TO CALCULATE YOUR RATES

The business of calculating rates, estimating income, invoicing and getting paid in a timely manner will go much more smoothly if you work out details and expectations ahead of time. When getting started, be sure to reserve enough time to research rates and calculate costs and earning requirements thoroughly. Here are some tips that will help you:

ESTABLISHING EARNING GOALS

Start by looking at how much you spend in a year. Sit down and analyze your bank accounts for the previous year to clearly see what you spent and where you were spending it. Based on that, you can project your costs for the following year. This allows you to set an earning goal, because you must cover your costs. Establishing goals for earning ties into looking at your market, the services you offer and your competition. It's a hugely complex and time-consuming process; no wonder people struggle to get started. But once you set a target, you'll know exactly what you're aiming for.

QUOTING

When you are quoting, you need to address your customers' requirements and preferences. If they are asking for a per-page rate, then that is what you need to give them. If they want a per-word rate (which is what you will encounter most often), then that's what they should get. However, it all boils down to your hourly rate. What you should be interested in is not whether it's X amount per word or two cents more; it's having a look at the text and estimating how many words you think you can do in an hour. Offer a rate based on that.

CALCULATING RATES

How much you make per hour determines whether you can accept a job or not, and whether it's profitable or not. It comes down to your yearly earning target. It's a little artificial, but to get started, think about what you want to make in 12 months. Let's say you want to make $24,000 (substitute the numbers with your currency) in the next 12 months. You would divide the $24,000 by 12. With 12 months in a year, you need to make $2000 a month. Divide that by four weeks in a month to get to $500 a week, which boils down to $100 a day. Then, imagine you want to work five hours a day; you would need to make $20 an hour. It's a bit of a silly example, but that is basically how to calculate an hourly rate. It all comes down to what you intend to earn in the next 12 months.

For your business to operate, you need to do other tasks in addition to translation. And for your business to be sustainable you need to be paid for those tasks in the same way you would if you were working for an employer. You wouldn't expect them to pay you for only the six hours you're translating, and to not pay you for the two hours that you're doing administration for them. You can be cheap for a few months, but then if you are not going to hit your earning target, you are not going to cover your costs, and there's no chance of continuing long term as a freelancer.

Another idea is to contact the translation associations in your country. They may provide a minimum rate per service list that could help you to get oriented on setting your rates. A lot of translators think that if they set their rates very low, they will have more work. This is not exactly true. They might get some work in the beginning, but they will have huge difficulties raising their rates to a normal standard afterwards. So, it is not advisable to market rates that are too low.

You can also check the ProZ.com website where a rate calculator and community rates are posted. This will give you an idea of the average rates as you are getting started.

From interview with Gwenydd Jones [www.translatorstudio.co.uk], *a Spanish-to-English professional translator with specialization in the business, marketing and legal fields.*

INVOICING AND GETTING PAID

The administrative work of invoicing and getting paid can sometimes get lost in the shuffle of managing projects and deadlines. But it should be an important part of your weekly routine, not only to ensure the maintenance of cash flow, but as a cornerstone of your organizational pride and professionalism.

BASIC INVOICING TIPS

- Everyone is different when it comes to administrative tasks such as invoicing. Some translators send invoices with their project files. It's a good practice, but always ask for a delivery receipt.

- Some clients have their own online invoicing systems where you can see whether the invoice has been accepted. You can check in the next day or so to get a status report on your payment.

- Localize your invoices to your foreign country. For European clients in particular, if you include the VAT (Value Added Tax) number, it helps them when dealing with their tax authorities.

OVERDUE INVOICES

Decide when you set up your business how you want to deal with overdue invoices. How many days are you going to wait before you send a reminder or ask about payment? It's a good policy to extend a 10-day grace period. But businesses use different accounting systems – some might be set up to do an accounts payable run once a week, while others might do it twice a month, or only once a month. If you happen to send in your invoice the day after they have paid all their vendors, there is likely going to be a period of waiting until they do their next run. If you are dealing with US or Canadian agencies and you are getting checks in the mail, you must allow for postal delays.

A first reminder for late payment should be friendly, just asking them to look into it. You will see what the response is, or if there is a response. If you don't get a response you probably have a problem. When you have bills that remain unpaid and they start getting old you end up in what is called a dunning process, which is sending repeat reminders. In the United States, dunning usually runs on a 30-, 60- and 90-day cycle. Let's say your client is 10 days late; you send a friendly reminder and receive a response saying the check will go out this week. The payment doesn't arrive, and is now 30 days late, so you send out your first dunning letter. It doesn't have to be paper mail; it can be an email, but with a slightly less friendly tone. Give them a fixed date to pay up. In some European countries, this is a requirement, otherwise the dunning notice is not considered legally valid.

The most common mistake new freelancers make is not checking payment policies with the client before accepting a project. The other most common reason for not getting paid in full is when there is dissatisfaction – the agency claims that the translator did not hold up their side of the bargain, or delivered a sub-par translation, or delivered late. And finally, you won't get paid if you don't submit your invoice – don't forget!

From interview with Ted Wozniak [www.tedwozniak.net], a US-based German-English translator, editor and proofreader.

WORKING WITH AGENCIES

Translators and interpreters just starting out will likely find their first clients through an agency. Even those with repeat customers and direct clients that constitute the bulk of their business, return to agency work from time to time.

WHERE TO FIND THE GOOD AGENCIES

The most effective way to discover the best agencies is through networking. Just ask your colleagues – they will be the most reliable source of information in terms of finding the agencies with which you want to work. If you are a member of an association that has corporate members, such as ITI or ATA, they can be a good initial source for established agency clients that abide by a code of conduct. Research association websites and check the ProZ.com Blue Board or the Payment Practices website [*www.paymentpractices.net*].

HOW TO CONTACT THEM

The first thing to do is to look at your target agency's website to see if they have a registration process and a form to fill in. If they provide a contact form, use it. Don't just send them your CV and completely ignore what they've requested on their website.

If there isn't a tab or a call to action that says "Freelance Translators Contact Us This Way," then write to them. Do not send them an almost anonymous email. Don't just write "Dear so and so, please find attached my CV" and then wait for them to contact you. You should find ways of making yourself attractive, because every agency sees hundreds of CVs daily. You have to make yours stand out.

If there is no contact protocol on your target agency's website, you need to find out to whom you should speak. The best thing to do is to call them and say, "This is who I am, and I am offering such and such, are you looking for a translator in my language combination or specialist areas?" While they may say no, they might add that they would love to have your details. Follow up immediately with the person to whom you have been speaking, or whoever they tell you to contact.

HOW CAN WE HELP AGENCIES FIND US?

It is more or less the same strategy whether you are looking for work from agencies or from direct clients: You have to be where they are going to look.

Make sure you are listed in the print or online directory of your national association. Clients will often look in the national or local translation association's directory. Being listed shows that you are professional and abide by a code of conduct.

Another place to be listed is in the online translation portals. When people are searching on Google, ProZ.com consistently throws up the most results, so having a profile there is important.

Having your own website, even if it's just a simple web page, is also very important. Recruiters looking for translators often go first to the ITI or ATA directory (or any other national association's directory). They give priority to people who have a website for the simple reason that it saves them a lot of time in making a phone call. They click on the link for the website and, if it's a good website, it will tell them everything they need to know about the person. Then they call or email to see if the translator is available and interested in the project that they have. A website tells a million stories and it can say a lot about you.

TEST TRANSLATIONS

Free test translations can be useful, but are not for everybody. When a company comes out of the blue and says we would like to work with you, but we want you to do this 1000-word test translation, be very wary (anything more than 500 words is too much). Before you accept or refuse to do the test, you should decide, is this a company I want to work with or not? What will I get out of it?

Be wary of very big companies who say they are recruiting translators in many different language combinations and they would like to put you on their books -- and for you to be on their books, you need to do a free sample translation. And you do it, and never hear from them again.

SIGNING CONTRACTS

Read contracts very carefully before signing them. If there's anything you're not happy with, especially related to payment terms or copyright, say so. All agreements are different, but they are always negotiable. If they are not, you might want to carefully consider if you want to work with them or not.

CREATING A FAVORABLE IMPRESSION

Number one – be friendly. This sounds obvious, but it is not. We are not always very friendly when dealing with agencies. A lot of translators work for agencies because they think they do not have a choice. They resent it and they resent the markup that agencies impose. If you do not want to work with translation agencies, then don't; just put all your efforts into finding direct clients. Otherwise, treat agencies like you would treat any other client.

Communicate. If you have a problem and you cannot meet a deadline, let the client know as soon as you can. We are all human beings, and we all make mistakes. Hell is not going to open just because your car broke down, you got stuck in a traffic jam or your child is ill and you cannot deliver. Just let the client know as soon as possible so they can find a backup solution. Even better, give them a backup solution. Get a colleague to help.

Also, be humble. When an agency comes to you and says there are some issues with your work, always take their constructive criticism graciously.

From interview with Anne de Freyman *[www.adf-translate.co.uk], a French translator based in the UK.*

WHAT DO AGENCIES LOOK FOR IN FREELANCE TRANSLATORS?

What qualifications are agencies looking for? If someone applies through an agency's website where they are asked to submit information, the agency will already have a good idea of the applicant's language combination, experience and so forth. They will look at the CV to make sure the candidate has the right qualifications, skills and experience. If the applicant claims to be a member of certain translation associations, that is verified, as are references. Talking to people who have already worked with the applicant gives a pretty good idea of the kind of professional they are. Translators should always check with their potential the person they are referring before passing on their details (and NEVER include those details on a CV), as some companies (not just translation agencies) may have a policy to not give references.

HOW DO AGENCIES DEAL WITH FALSE APPLICATIONS?

Unfortunately, there are still agencies unaware of this, but assuming they do, the first step is to check and then report the false application to the Translator Scammers Directory [www.translator-scammers.com/translator-scammers-directory.htm]. This is an invaluable resource that is doing a fantastic job exposing these scammers. If you come across translators who steal others' identities, you should likewise expose them and warn the real translator where possible.

WHAT NOT TO DO WHEN CONTACTING A TRANSLATION COMPANY

- Don't start cover letters with the generic "Dear Sir/Madam." It demonstrates that you are not actually interested in working with someone specific, but with anyone who'd reply. These days it is very easy to find out who you want to target, by checking social media profiles and doing a little bit of research. Of course, it may not always be possible (especially with large translation agencies), but it will definitely increase your chances.

- Don't ever badmouth clients. We can all get frustrated at times – whether it's because we haven't been paid on time, or because the source text wasn't as good as we would have liked it to be. But badmouthing clients on social media, or anywhere public, actually makes the translator look bad. Also, getting into arguments with other colleagues, bickering and always having a negative attitude – just don't. And for translators on social media, the "look at me" attitude is not attractive. We should be contributing something to the general discussion and not just promoting ourselves.

WHAT TO DO WHEN CONTACTING A TRANSLATION COMPANY

- We are overwhelmed with choice when it comes to social media. We've got so many channels we can use – Twitter, Facebook, and Google+. Every translator should have a website or a blog, though not all do. If you don't want to have a blog, at least have a Facebook page. If you have something interesting to say and you want to write a longer post, you can also use Google+.

- If you use Twitter in your professional capacity as a translator and you want to find clients this way, make sure you put your language combination or specialization in your profile.

- Being responsive is always a plus. Not all projects are urgent, but most clients appreciate it when a translator gets back to them quickly. Whether or not you are interested in a particular project, or whether or not you have time, one of the things that we can do to stand out is to be responsive and very pleasant to work with in general.

- It's important to invest time and energy in keeping existing clients. Some ways to do that, apart from delivering quality work, are to respond quickly and always follow up. This beneficial marketing tip works very well.

- Following up after you've delivered a project is important. Wait a couple of days and check in to get feedback and see whether the clients are happy. They may have questions, or maybe they want some amendments to the translation. Clients will be impressed by the fact that you have followed up, and that makes for a very good working relationship.

From interview with Alina Cincan

[www.inboxtranslation.com/about/alina-cincan], a UK-based translator and interpreter, and Managing Director of Inbox Translation.

CHAPTER 2 – GETTING CLIENTS

Finding, getting and keeping clients should be an ongoing daily activity for translators at all points in their career. This chapter features tips on everything from personal branding that will send the right message to agencies and potential customers, to how to network and find new clients, to the fine art of effectively communicating with clients once you are working with them. Again, I've collected established international translators' and marketing experts' practical advice gleaned from my podcast Marketing Tips for Translators *– find out more about these translation professionals at the end of each section.*

It's very important for translators, especially those who freelance, to take control of the way they live their professional lives. You don't want to feel like you're a victim, or that you are forced to put up with bad practices from certain agencies or low levels of rates. You want to feel completely free to decide what you want to specialize in, how you want to approach your clients, how many clients you want to find, and whether they are direct or agency clients.

YOU ARE IN CHARGE

You're the one in charge. You take responsibility for what happens to you, and if unfortunate events happen to you, you bounce back. You learn a lesson. If something goes wrong, you may decide not to do the same thing next time. Essentially, it's your decision and these things are in your hands. Obviously, we've all been subjected to a client who suddenly disappears without paying. That is not in your hands, but your reaction to that situation is, and so too is the way you deal with your next client. You can manage your relationships with agencies so that you're viewed not as some kind of employee, but as an equal partner.

Some translators with huge talent undercharge because they are not confident. And other translators with less talent may earn more money because they have a certain kind of approach and they take control of each relationship. The key is authenticity. Each of us is different. We have different specialties, backgrounds, values, needs, family situations, and above all, different interests and passions and skills. It's essential for the freelance translator to reflect on exactly what kind of job they want to take on so they don't simply get swept along in whatever work lands on their desk.

AGENCIES, DIRECT CLIENTS, OR BOTH

Some translators may really want to work with agencies, because they feel comfortable in that type of relationship. These people know themselves and that's excellent. Other people want to have a mixture of agency work (to provide a little bit of security when things go quiet) and direct clients. Others deal only with direct clients, perhaps because they have a more entrepreneurial profile. We need to ask ourselves, "What do I want to do?" You will never get translators to agree on whether direct clients or agencies are better.

When you look at people and the way they behave online, you can learn quite a lot about their character without ever meeting them. Try to practice a set of attitudes towards your colleagues and clients, whether they are agencies or direct, that is based on tolerance and respect and a willingness to be flexible. That capacity to see your clients as partners and collaborators is important, as is the right to say no to things that leave you feeling uninspired or restless. Procrastination is a signal from your body and mind that you need to change. Procrastination is feedback that says something is not going right for you. Think about it, work on it and change it.

LOOKING AT OUR ATTITUDE

Most of our focus as translators is on marketing, improving our competence and the skills needed to do the job. We talk a lot about quality, we talk a lot about websites, and we talk a lot about technical tools such as CAT tools.

Without competence, without quality work, without a reasonable command of the tools and a very high command of the languages, you might as well change your job. These features constitute the basis for anything that we do. However, that's not enough. These things account for only about 25% of our potential to achieve.

The other 75% relates to attitude – with the way we go about doing things, the way we focus our energy on our work, and the way we deal with everything that happens to us on a daily basis. It also relates to the way we project ourselves, the impressions we create with clients and with colleagues. We can assume that most of the people we see working online are committed and skilled and that they have all the necessary tools. However, when you look at the range of translators across the board, you see people who are just surviving and you see people who are thriving. Both kinds of translator have similar levels of linguistic competence, so what is the difference between those people?

If people would add the right kind of attitude and mentality to their basic competence, they could reach 90%-95% of their potential. Conversely, there are people with the basic 25% who use their remaining 75% in a negative way. They feel so hostile towards their clients and colleagues that they actually undermine their own ability, and sabotage their own possibility of success. They've got the skills, but they're not finding work because of their attitude or perhaps their lack of confidence. Or maybe they're just not in the right job.

ATTITUDE AND CLIENTS

In terms of our attitude towards clients, being extremely pleasant and building relationships with them and going the extra mile where possible (which might mean the occasional pro bono or urgent overnight job) will pay off. If you have a question, pick up the phone. Because we work in isolation, sometimes we forget to use that human side. Essentially our job is about communication; it's about getting meaning across and it's a human thing. We work with words and phrases and meanings, but essentially, it's one human being talking to another through the text. Sometimes we get our heads buried in the text and lose sight of that human element.

From interview with Andrew Morris [www.andrewmorris.fr], a translator and writer based in France.

What does your network really look like? In many cases it will consist of colleagues you've gotten to know at industry events. Your clients are part of your network, as are like-minded people with whom you don't actually do any business, but with whom you stay in touch to exchange contacts, ideas, and the like.

It is worthwhile for translators to keep tight relationships with the advertising and marketing sectors. They are the ones making websites and designing campaigns for their clients, and they are the ones with clients who want to go international. These connections can be fruitful if you clarify expectations on both sides, don't exploit the relationship and honor honesty. Even just talking to those with whom you'd like to work can be beneficial.

From interview with Marta Stelmaszak

[www.wantwords.co.uk/martastelmaszak], a communications specialist who provides content strategy and translation services between Poland and English-speaking countries.

Effective communication is both a means to achieve your business goals and the very essence of our business. Have you ever experienced being a bit unsure about what the client really wants, or not having kept good records of your interactions with a client so you don't remember what you or the client promised? If so, your communication with clients could be improved.

Communication is not only talking – it is also written communication (even texting, or what we post on Twitter). When I first started out, I focused solely on the actual translation part of doing my job. Producing high-quality translation is still the cornerstone of my business, but I have noticed that if I pay attention to communication, I can create a more profitable relationship with my clients and colleagues.

TURNAROUND TIME

One of the most frequent requests to translators is for fast turnaround. Clients always seem to need things yesterday. Either the customer wants a quick service in order to create lots of content to be published quickly, or they need to feel that they are important enough for top priority. These people may react very differently to the options you propose to them. While figuring this out may take some time, you will see that there are only a fixed number of typical behaviors, so it does get easier.

OTHER NEEDS CUSTOMERS MAY HAVE

Lots of people have bad experiences with translation services. They may come to you after having tried a machine-translated option, or a bulk translation option that proved to be unsatisfactory. These people have felt the pain of not getting a quality product. In such cases you might, for example, offer to partner with another translator to ensure their files are proofread twice. This may make them feel more secure about the outcome of your work – and then you will have a satisfied customer.

You may find that some clients don't really understand translation when they come to you for a translation. They might need to be educated, or they might feel a bit ashamed of not knowing much and want to intervene in or be part of the process. You may need to make them feel they are part of a team.

THE VALUES YOU OFFER

As well as listening actively and asking the right questions, you can offer clients your experience and your understanding of what's going on beyond the text. For example, in order to translate the text of a machinery manual, you also need to understand how the machinery works. Your understanding of your client's industry is a value. You can't possibly know about everything and anything, but let's say if you are a legal translator and you translate a contract, you understand the words of the contract, but also the laws that regulate the contract. That is an asset because you can spot grey areas, or you're able to tell your client which standard term will make a text clearer, for example. We have a tendency to focus on the price of our work, but this is not the only thing we have to offer. When you quote, you quote so many things about your work – price is just one factor.

- Determine your client's communication style. Does the client prefer you to pick up the phone, or send a quick email, or do they want to meet you face to face? Try to adapt to your client's preferred style if possible.

- Keep records of your interactions. You can do this by adding everything to an Excel worksheet, saving emails, and taking notes during phone conversations or meetings that you later send as a summary. This will make it easy to see with whom you need to check in or follow up.

- Pay attention to your tone – especially in email. Always remember to keep it professional (one good tip is to always reread the email before sending it), and pay attention to tone, style, grammar and typos. Make sure your voicemail also has a professional-sounding message. Always treat the client with respect.

- Be very specific about documenting project terms and expectations in advance. If you don't know, ask, and have everything documented in writing. If you don't like to talk on the phone you can, for example, set appointments for communication so you can be more prepared when you communicate. I sometimes screen incoming calls, letting it go to voicemail, and then call back as soon as I have prepared what I want to say. If you are following up with a client, ask if you can call back at a specific time, or offer an alternative time to talk.

- Focus on listening to what the client says instead of thinking ahead in the conversation. This is mostly useful for phone calls, but it can also be a powerful tool for negotiating rates. Usually in negotiations, if you remain quiet, the client might think what they are offering is too low and give you a new offer.

- Respond quickly. In order for us to provide great customer service we need to make an effort to return emails and phone calls promptly, within an hour or so if possible. That makes us seem easy and professional to work with. If you are unavailable, remember to activate away messages on all of your communication channels – email, voicemail, Skype, etc. It shows that you care about the caller's business.

- Be available. Being a freelancer means setting your own hours, but if you want to work with a client, you need to be available based on their schedule. Informing clients of your time zone is also important.

- Try to identify your next step in advance. Make your process as clear as possible for you and your clients. When you accept a job, ask the client to confirm with a P.O. number before you get started (for agencies), or to confirm with a contract for direct clients. To make it easier for the client, you can include your price or fee when you confirm the deadline, which tools to use, etc., so it is easy for the client to confirm those terms as well.

- Make a template of the first emails that you send to clients that clarify the scope of the project. This will save you a lot of time and eventually money. The projects you will work on may differ, but the initial stages are mostly the same for every project. So a template will help you ensure that you did not leave out anything important or forget something, while at the same time recording details about the work.

- When delivering a job, remember to ask the client for feedback and ask them if you can help them with a future project. Or, simply say that you are looking forward to working with them again.

- Keep the client in the loop. If you are working on a long-term or large project, send the client updates weekly, or daily, to keep them informed. It is your responsibility to apprise them of the project status. Different clients may expect different levels of contact, so try to find out how often your client wants you to provide an update. Even if it seems a little excessive, you could send one or two email updates letting the customer know that everything is going as planned, or that you are a little bit ahead or behind.

- Confront problems. Do not send an email five minutes before the deadline with a lot of questions on the file, or say that it will be delayed. If you are being delayed, make sure to inform the client as soon as possible so they can make arrangements. As problems arise, deadlines may shift or revisions may get out of hand, but you must communicate with the client to find the solution.

- Verify everything by repeating and recording it in writing. Even if you agree on something over the phone, always send an email with details that the client can verify or confirm. Ask, don't assume. If your invoice is not paid, or if you are unsure of something, just ask.

- Always keep things positive. Don't take your horrible day out on your client, and don't let an angry client get to you. You can keep the conversation positive and focus on finding a solution instead. This applies not only to how we communicate in emails or on the phone, but to everything we post online. Many agencies and direct clients tell me that before they hire someone they Google them and check out their presence on social media. What you share online can be seen by anyone, so it is important to be aware of the image you're presenting.

From solo episode with Tess Whitty [*www.marketingtipsfortranslators.com/episode-70-effective-communication-skills-for-translators*] *and From interview with Alessandra Martelli* [*www.mtmtranslations.com*], *a translator, copywriter and trainer based in Turin, Italy.*

The Get Clients Now! ™ program is a detailed 28-day daily marketing plan that gives you a list of things to do, and tells you exactly when to do them. The power of the program comes from its simplicity. Anyone can create an effective plan and put it into motion immediately – even if they have never marketed a business before.

An effective program to market your professional services can be divided into just six strategies. In order of effectiveness, they are: direct contact and follow-up, networking and referral building, public speaking, writing and publicity, promotional events and advertising. The first three are the most effective actions to market your company as a self-employed professional. These strategies push you to establish personal contact with new clients or with people who can lead you to prospective clients. They build credibility and trust. When you put direct contact, increased credibility, and building trust together, you have a really powerful combination to make your marketing more effective.

You no longer have any need to be located where your clients are; many translators do business virtually. You can interact with the people who are going to become your clients by email, phone, online chat, or through social media. You can speak to them in virtual ways – a podcast, or a telecast or webinar. You can interact with them online, or by text. There are so many ways of being in contact with potential clients or referral sources that have nothing to do with interacting in person.

MARKETING PIPELINE

The marketing pipeline is the central feature of what she would call the universal marketing cycle. It is the cycle that every professional must follow to get clients, no matter the line of business. It is a diagnostic tool; it helps you to determine exactly where you need to focus in your marketing.

Begin by filling your marketing pipeline with prospects, contacts, leads and referrals. These people will flow through your pipeline into your follow-up pool. When you follow up with them, you are attempting to persuade them to have a sales conversation in which you ask them what they need, you tell them how you can help, and then you see if there is a match between you. Then you close the sale. At any given time, your marketing may be stuck in one of these basic stages: filling the pipeline, following up, having sales conversations or closing a sale. Understanding them will help you to determine exactly where the emphasis should be in your marketing right now.

SUCCESS INGREDIENTS

The way to discover your missing ingredients for success is to ask yourself why you cannot fill your marketing pipeline. The answer to that question will tell you what is missing. You might not be clear on who your best clients might be – in that case a success ingredient for you would be to create a market niche defining who to approach.

Or, you might think that your website does not showcase your current abilities, so your success ingredient might be an updated website. You could be nervous about reaching out to people you do not know, in which case your success ingredient might be self-confidence skills.

What this process does is point you towards a specific tool, project or a skill set you need to be working on in order to get rid of the obstacles to successful marketing.

In the Get Clients Now! system you end up with a list of specific things to do on a regular basis, preferably daily, that are directly aimed at getting clients. This is your action plan. The actions in the plan are organized by the stage of the universal marketing cycle on which you have chosen to focus. That is why it is so important to go through the diagnostic process first. There are so many different things you can do to market yourself. How do you know what you should be doing right now? Knowing which stage of the marketing cycle needs more work can guide you to picking the right actions to address your personal issues in your unique situation. Let's say you choose follow-up as the stage where you need to put more effort. If you look at the action plan menu of the Get Clients Now program, you might see choices like call three prospects or referral sources every day, or add ten new names to my in-house mailing list daily, or have lunch or coffee with a prospect once a week. Any of these options can help you with the goal of better follow-up with prospective clients.

CHOOSING MARKETING ACTIVITIES

The activities you choose depend on the stage of the marketing cycle on which you are focusing, and on the marketing strategies you have determined are going to be the most effective for you. Is it focusing on networking, or referral building, or is your focus right now on direct contact and follow-up? Which activities do you prefer and feel more natural to you? If you choose activities that you actually like doing, rather than those you would rather avoid, you are going to do them. Don't just put them on a to-do list and never get them done.

Over 50% of the people who follow the Get Clients Now! program are stuck in the two stages of filling the marketing pipeline and following up. The remaining 45-50% are focusing on having conversations around closing sales. There are a few critical elements to keep in mind during any of these stages. The first is to be intentional; do not just choose to fill the pipeline by randomly going to a networking event or joining any old online community. Who are your ideal clients, the ones you really want the most, where are those people, what could you do to fill the pipeline with them as opposed to just any possible prospect? Do not follow up with whatever name happens across your desk today. Who are your hot prospects, the ones that you really want? That is where your efforts should go; be intentional.

The first thing to do is to define any missing success ingredients. Let's say you aren't sure about your niche. Part of your program can be to get really clear on what your market niche is. You can find more information than you could possibly want on how to create a market niche definition with a Google search. Put that desired success ingredient into your plan, then spend an hour a day for the next week defining your market niche. You can do the same for any other ingredients for success you might be missing.

Secondly, stay organized – this is so critical. If you organize your contacts into high, medium and low, or hot, warm and cold, you can better identify with whom to follow up. If you capture every possible prospect or referral source that comes into your world, you have a much better sense of whether your pipeline is full or not, or if it is lopsided and you have too many people in this category while you need more in that category. Being organized is underrated as a strategy, but it is critical to effective marketing. Have an organized way to keep track of who you know, who you do not know yet, and how and when you have been in touch with those people.

Allow yourself to be persistent. You are not bugging people if you follow up with them regularly; you are being professional and showing consistency. If you talk to someone and they say they cannot use you right now, but they have a project coming up next month and they might be able to use you then, write that date down, follow up with them, and do not think that someone will call you when they need you – it doesn't work that way. The person they are going to call is the last translator who was in touch with them, not the one they talked to a month ago. And when you have not been in touch with someone yet, but you have good reason to believe that they could use you, follow up again and again. You are not bugging people, you are showing that you are professional and consistent.

One way to follow up is just to call someone and ask if they are ready to work with you yet. But there are a lot of other possibilities. Getclientsnow.com has an article called 44 Ways to Follow Up with Your Prospects. One of the points it makes is that following up does not have to be just a phone call. It can be sending the person an interesting article that you ran across and thought would be helpful or useful to them. It could be letting them know about an upcoming event, or anything that keeps your name in front of them and reminds them that they know a translator to contact the next time they have a project in Swedish or whatever your specialty is.

From interview with C.J. Hayden *[www.getclientsnow.com], a business coach, trainer, and speaker, and author of* Get Clients Now! Get Hired Now! The One-Person Marketing Plan Workbook, and 50 Ways Coaches Can Change the World.

FACE-TO-FACE NETWORKING

Face-to-face networking is interacting live with other humans. It can be so much more satisfying than activities like cold calling. Networking is really just making connections with other people and trying to nurture those connections into meaningful relationships. You don't want to miss out on paying work or opportunities. You don't want to miss that email or that phone call. However, when you're offering professional services such as translation, the payback from face-to-face networking is just huge compared to other things you can do. Networking is free. It pretty much costs only a little bit of your time, a little bit of a method, and getting up enough courage to put yourself out there.

HOW TO NETWORK

When you're networking, you're not selling. You're just getting out there meeting contacts and building relationships that will ultimately turn into referrals, or maybe even turn directly into customers. You're not there to sign a deal with anybody on the spot; remembering this can take the pressure down a few notches. Just be yourself and be authentic and get out there, and help other people make connections too. If you know two people you think could do business together, introduce them. It's really good for your networking karma. People generally crave more face-to-face interaction these days, and anything you can do to cultivate more of it is going to set you apart from other service providers.

GET OVER THE FEAR

You know the importance of networking face-to-face, but how can you improve the experience? To some degree, most people are a little bit uncomfortable with it, and the biggest type of excuse seems to be that they don't know anybody and they don't have a network. But even people who say they don't know anyone probably know around 400 people when they start making a list. What's really at issue is our fear of putting ourselves out there and being visible. You may be worried that people won't like you, or that people won't want to buy your services. We put a lot of unnecessary pressure on ourselves.

WHAT NETWORKS TO FOCUS ON

As a translator specifically, you should focus on three networks. The first network is your professional peer group, and it's probably the easiest one to cultivate. Where do you find professional peers? Translation associations, interpreter associations – find the professional association for your specialty and get involved. Volunteer. Go to events. Go to training sessions or workshops.

If you are like a lot of translators, you want to start diversifying the types of customers with which you work. Referrals are a safe way to get new clients. Another potential network is the circle in which your potential customers move. That could be Chamber of Commerce-related groups, industry-specific associations, and similar organizations. Your specialty areas and your customers' industries and markets are extremely varied, so there's no general rule. You have to seek out potential customers with the right fit.

Another potential network is personal – your family, your kids' school, other parents, neighbors, fellow alumni from your college, friends. Everyone you know is a potential member of your network.

When you talk to people at family gatherings, or at neighborhood gatherings or events with friends, get people to talk about what they do and really listen to them.

FOCUS ON HELPING

You are not out there to sell; you are there to give. This mindset makes attending a networking event much easier. And once you're there, you will find nice people to talk to; it's just fun and very fascinating. People should not feel like they're alone in having that hesitant feeling, because everybody has that feeling to some extent. And if you go back to that exhaustive list of everyone you know, you can actually rate each contact by how warm or cold they are. For example, warm would be how comfortable you feel, like you could pick up the phone and call them right now. Doing this can also help you overcome some of those mental barriers you might have to networking.

BEFORE THE EVENT

Do your homework. Figure out who you want to meet and Google that person. Google the company and read about what they have been doing. That way, when you do meet them, you can have an intelligent initial conversation with them. Have a game plan, and be ready to execute your plan when you actually get there.

Prepare some small talk, something to mention about the weather, or a local sports team, or something about the organization that's hosting the event. Avoid topics of politics and religion. Someone mentioned once in a session that she had met somebody whose company tells salespeople headed to some sort of event or conference to read People magazine first. Also make sure that you have enough business cards.

You have to be realistic about your objectives for attending events. Keep them attainable. Put a specific number on them. Actually list the people you want to meet and try to find your pathway to them. Your success is of higher quality if you connect with these few people, and have meaningful conversations with them. You want to cultivate quality over quantity.

DURING THE EVENT

Be sure to arrive on time – there is no such thing as being fashionably late. When you get there and you're alone and not sure if you know people, hang around the refreshments area where there will be lots of traffic. Sitting down somewhere and waiting for someone to come and sit next to you and keep you company usually doesn't work. You have to be a little bit proactive, so make sure you're not sitting down.

If you see a single person just standing there, go up and just smile, be friendly. They may be looking for someone to talk with too, so introduce yourself. If everyone is grouped up already, look for groups of three or more people. Usually when there are two people, they're having a conversation with each other and it's probably not the best idea to walk in on that. When there are three or more in a group, there is generally going to be some sort of opening; just walk up, don't interrupt, but wait until someone stops talking and welcomes you into the group – and then introduce yourself.

I'm sure you've all been in a situation where you've been talking to someone and the person is looking all around for someone more important or interesting to talk to. When you're at these events and you're networking with somebody, the person that you're engaging with should be the most important person in the room. That's common courtesy and respect.

If you are a shy person and lack confidence in these situations, you can go into the bathroom or somewhere no one is going to see you and just put a really big grin on your face. Smile broadly for a minute or so, and it will create a higher level of dopamine in your system, which will get you more relaxed and increase your confidence and positive attitude when you finally get into the main room.

A power pose can also be very helpful; there's a really great TED talk on that with Amy Cuddy – Your Body Language Shapes Who You Are). It's a way of being very expansive in the way you're standing in the room. It projects a certain confidence and power.

Try not to drink too much alcohol. You don't want to start slurring your words, or stumbling around, or saying things that are distasteful. Be careful with humor, with your jokes. It's good to be funny if you are naturally funny, or if you have a couple of good jokes (and it's always great to know several jokes that you can pull out in different contexts) – people really appreciate that.

If you have found somebody and you're comfortable talking to them, don't monopolize them. They may want to get away, and if you're there to network you want to meet as many people as you can in the evening. Know when to leave. Wait until someone else comes into the group, that's a great time to exit. If they are an acquaintance, you can introduce them and excuse yourself, and now those two people are talking. It's a lot harder to step away when you're just talking to one person.

FOLLOW-UP

- No matter what type of interaction you had, just follow up. Whatever you told a contact that you would do, do it. Ninety-nine percent of people do not. So it will make a really good impression if you are the one percent that follows up.

- Keep track of contacts. An Excel spreadsheet, even for advanced networkers, can be a very powerful tool. Or use a CRM (a customer relationship management program). You can use it for invoices, you can integrate it with email marketing, and you can set alerts if you want to be in touch with contacts every six months just to say hello. You just need a tool that lets you sort and categorize information and work with it.

- A lot of us with small service-oriented businesses operate in feast or famine mode. We're so busy doing production for our customers we don't have time to keep leads in the pipeline. And then we have a downturn in work because we haven't been nurturing our leads. Networking is a way to quickly find work. Maybe you just delivered a big project and you don't have anything lined up. Potential clients are part of your network, so begin there.

- If you specialize in marketing translation or pharmaceutical translation, you might want to specifically target those industries and try to cultivate your network around people working in those fields. Like any goal, you should break it down into steps. Write an email or phone script inviting someone to lunch to help develop your network, or see if a warm contact can introduce you to anybody in the marketing or pharmaceutical fields. You must break things down into specific actionable items, otherwise you're not going to achieve your goals.

From interview with Sara Freitas [www.sfmtraduction.com/en/sara-freitas] *a professional French to English marketing translator, English copywriter and founder of SFM Traduction, and* **from interview with John Di Rico** [www.johndirico.com], *a specialist in financial translation and marketing from French to English who also offers training to professional translators.*

PRICING STRATEGIES

Seventy percent of the respondents to a recent survey I conducted thought finding higher-paying clients was the hardest part of starting out in translation. The second-hardest was setting prices for services. However, once you figure out your target per hour income and decide how many hours you can work, you can base your project prices on these numbers quite easily. Or set a pricing range so you can be a bit flexible with your rates and leave some room for negotiation.

PRICING ZONES

You might have already noticed in your translation career that you can complete some jobs faster and generate more income per hour, whereas others are slower and generate less income per hour. You could set different prices for different jobs if you wanted to and still get the same per-hour income by developing different price zones. These help us determine whether we should take on a job or not, or perhaps try to negotiate the rate.

One way to look at it is to imagine green, yellow and red price zones. Green rates are premium rates. As long as the job is not too difficult, or looks like it will not take too long, we should try not to turn down a green zone job as long as it is within our expertise.

The yellow zone price is when the rate offered is our minimum rate. It's not an ideal rate, but it is worth considering. Perhaps the job is very easy, or fast, and we can earn good money. Or perhaps it has been a bit slow on the work front lately and we need to take it on to earn some money that week or month. It could also be a really interesting and fun project where we can learn something or develop a new skill.

If the price offered dips down into the red zone, we should turn it down. We must have a red zone in order to have a viable business and make ends meet. But what if we said yes to a project in the red zone only to be so booked up that we did not have time to take on a better paying project, or to market to the clients that pay better? In the long run, we're better off turning down these projects. Try to market to better-paying clients instead.

EXTRA CHARGES AND DISCOUNTS

Extra fees can be charged for rush assignments. Take this into account when you negotiate prices.

Some clients may ask you for volume discounts on a per-project or a per-client basis. This is more common if you work with agencies, especially with fuzzy matches and repetitions when you need to use computer translation tools. Always make sure you can still earn enough to cover your costs. For example, discounts on a per-project basis can be considered if you will increase your output during the course of the project because you become more familiar with the subject (in particular, terminology) and work faster.

You can also offer a discount to particular clients, but this is almost never a good idea. You might get a steady stream of jobs coming in, but if they are at discounted rates and make you unavailable to work for better-paying clients, it isn't worth it. Many agencies ask for CAT-tool-based discounts (these are for repetitions and hundred percent matches using Computer Aided Translation tools).

Such requests for discounts are quite common, but we should give some thought before saying yes to them, since it can mean a significant reduction in income and reduce the benefits of our investment in that tool. The amount of discount should be proportional to the productivity gains you get from using the tool. My basic advice is that if the job still covers your costs and you can reach your target per-hour rate, it's OK if you really want the job. But I know several translators who never give any CAT-tool-based discounts, and this is usually not an issue at all if you work with direct clients.

BY THE WORD, HOUR OR PROJECT?

Of the different rate options we have, the most common at agencies is to charge by the word. Direct clients usually don't know what that means; however, it is still the norm in our industry and in the agency market.

The advantage here is that if you charge by the source word, everyone knows in advance exactly how much the translation is going to cost before the project even starts. The disadvantage is that billing by the word makes translation seem like a commodity. Per-word billing also discourages us from doing thorough research, because we're not earning money for doing the research, we're just earning for each word we translate. Another option is to charge by the hour. This is simple and easy to negotiate and rush rates can be established. If it is a time-sensitive job, an hourly rate can also be adjusted to make up for changes in the job scope, for example if the client adds material to the translation, or if it takes a lot longer than anticipated.

The disadvantage is that clients may be wary that there is no fixed price or ceiling price. Interestingly, most translation agencies seem to be resistant to paying the hourly rate that is equivalent to what we make when we bill by the word.

Unless we have a very good handle on the translation speed for every document, or unless our clients will agree to start a project without a binding quote, knowing exactly how to estimate a job on a per-hour basis can be very difficult. Another popular option among freelance professionals is to use project fees. These can be tailored to match the scope of the job and enable us to predict our income more easily. This method has the advantage of allowing us to tweak the per-word or per-hour rate without discussing the details with the client. It also gives the client one number to focus on, and they don't need to worry about words or hours. I usually give a project price to my direct clients. The disadvantage of using project rates is that it's also difficult for us to calculate how long it will take. If your client tries to add on extras to the project, you might have to renegotiate, which can get tricky. Another disadvantage is that we get locked into this fixed bid, and there is no wiggle room if the project takes twice as long as expected.

PACKAGE PRICING

Package pricing is to place several products or services together in a single package deal. The package usually includes one big ticket item and at least one complementary item or service. For example, for XXX you get translation and proofreading by me, for XXX you get translation and proofreading by me, plus proofreading by a second native professional, and for XXX you also get complete formatting. The advantage of package pricing is that it can be posted publicly on your website or in your brochure for all to see. That makes it more difficult for clients trying to bargain you down. It can also be helpful for clients you know well. They can select from a menu of prices that allows them more control. The disadvantage is that there is less flexibility when it comes to a challenging project or client.

Direct clients are used to paying in a variety of ways; however, they're usually not used to per-word rates, which they find confusing. You can do them a favor by charging by the project hour or even use a day rate. The further you get away from per-word pricing, the better for this type of client.

NEGOTIATING YOUR PRICES

As a business owner, you have to make some tough decisions – including walking away from work that does not pay what you charge. There will always be clients looking for world-class quality, but who are not very price-sensitive. But if you charge adequate rates, you do not need hundreds of clients, you just need a few good repeat customers. Most discussions about rates involve an element of negotiation. The better you are at negotiating your price, the better your rates will be. The first and easiest negotiation tip to remember is to reduce the scope of your work in the project, rather than reducing the rate. This acts as a first line of defense for your rates and helps ensure that you do not do more for less. For example, when negotiating a project with a client, price isn't the only thing on the table. You can discuss deadlines, delivery methods, communication preferences, and other options. The more variables you can negotiate, the higher the likelihood that both parties will feel like winners.

Another tip is to try not to be the first to suggest a number. Instead, wait for a quote proposed by the client. The other party often has much more information than you do. Wait for the client to state their budget, and then start the negotiation. Establish the lowest rate you can accept and don't budge. Don't go into the red zone. Of course, we must always be ready to walk away from a negotiation if it's not going to work out. A good way to make sure we are ready to walk away is to have a buffer of savings. That way, when the jobs are few and far between, we don't have to agree to something just because we're desperate to get some money and pay our bills. If we do sometimes accept a lower rate for a project, it's important to remind the client that this is an exception and it's for this project only. Don't establish the precedent of a lower price for that client.

RAISING YOUR RATES

I continually raised my rate a little every year for the first five to six years I was working as a freelance translator. Many clients stayed with me, some disappeared, and some new ones were added to my roster. These days I find that I've reached a ceiling with agencies and getting higher rates is a little bit more difficult, unless I find new clients. Many agencies don't like rate increases, but it isn't impossible. So how can we increase our income without raising our current rates? One strategy is to quote reasonably high from the start. Another is to raise rates only when you approach new agencies and have nothing to lose. Once the upper ceiling that agencies generally impose is reached, the only ways to get a higher income are to move on to direct clients or to become more efficient.

If you do want to try to raise your rates for existing clients, the best time to do it is when you're really busy. Or, you could do a minimal increase at the beginning of each year to adjust for inflation. A cent or two a year, for example, is usually acceptable. Give a good heads-up before raising rates and explain exactly why you are raising your rates (for inflation, or because you have upgraded your tools, or gained a new specialization or certification). For agencies with which you haven't worked in a long time, send your current rates and see how they react. You can rationalize the rate increase by pointing out that most of your other clients are now paying you X amount of whichever currency, and that for you to be able to continue to prioritize them as a client, you would like to ask them to meet your current rate. This will make sense to clients, and it's polite – which opens the door for negotiation. That said, if you want to increase your rates, you must always realize that it's a negotiation you might lose.

From solo episode by Tess Whitty
[www.marketingtipsfortranslators.com/episode-30-tips-pricing-strategies-negotiation-raising-prices-translators]

There are plenty of ways to price and sell a translation service. Value pricing is one strategy that stands out. If your client is like a design agency or an IT consultancy that normally outsources work and is used to paying a day rate or an hourly rate to their outsourced staff, then you'll have no trouble implementing any one of these slightly different strategies. It will probably save you time, and make you more money in the long run, to charge a day or project rate rather than charging per word.

As an industry, we need to sell translation as an investment for the client, and position ourselves to help them find new markets or make sales. It is more important to understand what they're trying to do than for them to understand what we're trying to do, which is to enjoy the translation and make it as accurate and clear to read as possible. Understanding the client's goals can save you time in all sorts of ways, and it can also help you with pricing.

Day rate is a magic phrase with most clients, because that's what they're charged by most of their other providers. Consultants are more project-based, but if you're looking at similar professions to our own – copywriters, designers, freelancers – they are hired on a contract basis. That's the way to go on certain projects, and it's a very interesting way to make the most of an opportunity as it arises, especially when you have to try to educate the client on per-word pricing. If you just give them something they're used to, there's never any question about that.

- Cycle out the worst clients and start spending more time on the best.

- Make yourself as productive as possible so that you can either spend more time working, if that's what you want to do, or spend less time working for similar levels of income. Spending time arguing over the trivial details of a translation, the per-word price, for example, or even amendments to the translation that you've done, is a bit of a waste of time – because you could be spending that time working. Sometimes it's better to just accept the changes – unless they're horrendous, of course – and move on. Do not spend too much time being a perfectionist.

- Ask the client to sum up their notes and revision requests in a single email. If they are willing, this could save you a lot of time.

From interview with Luke Spear [www.lukespear.co.uk], a UK-based French-to-English translator specializing in IT, automotive and marketing copy.

When you first get started with direct clients, and you only have one client, you may think it's a fluke or luck. When you have three direct clients, the number is sufficient to give you confidence. The last thing you want to do is get overwhelmed while building your business. So contain your first direct clients to a manageable number – three is enough to get comfortable, but it also establishes a trend.

THREE ACTION STEPS TO REACH THESE FIRST DIRECT CLIENTS

- You must know who your direct clients are going to be – you have to identify them. If you don't know who they are, you can't reach them.

- You must know how to reach them on a large scale. Determine what this group of people has in common so you can reach out to them in large numbers.

- Reach out to those people – whether it's business owners or other service providers – who are already selling to your target market. You're not direct competition to them, but you are serving the same market. Based on your specialization or your background, you can think about who you want to work with and create a marketing persona.

TIPS FOR REACHING THE LARGE NUMBERS

Newsletters are a very powerful tool, not only to establish credibility, but to tell everyone that you're going to be around for a long time. Newsletters can also help you build a list of potential clients. When you contact them, it won't seem odd to ask them for work; instead it will feel more like relationship-building.

There are different ways to entice potential clients to join your newsletter list. For a new client you might compliment something they have done, or make a suggestion and, if they have time, make an appointment to talk further.

Conduct regular informational interviews with your existing clients, take them out for a coffee or something and just ask them for advice. Sometimes they will offer referrals. This kind of meeting can reveal a lot of information, so never underestimate the power of having a casual informational interview with a client.

USING OTHER SERVICE PROVIDERS

Piggybacking on service providers or business owners that are already serving your target market is a useful strategy. A lot of translators underestimate the power of building these kinds of strategic partnerships. What you can do is approach them, but come from a place of support. Come across as someone who wants to help and you're likely to get a response.

Let's say I'm a Chinese/English translator and you are Swedish/English translator. We are not serving the same market, but we can serve a broader market together. It's possible for us to form a strategic alliance with other service providers such as freelance writers, web designers, business consultants, lawyers and marketers. Our target markets may need these complementary services, but they don't have them readily available. We can get together to provide them.

Another strategy is to try to help businesses using translation services to have a better business. You don't want to come across as a know-it-all; you just want to be helpful. Most people have received unsolicited emails from web designers or marketers that say they can do this or that for your website. It can be annoying. Without providing background information or having any existing rapport, you likely won't get much response with this approach. But, if you can provide a critique in a limited but very positive way, they may come back to you for more. Finally, instead of coming across as begging for business, you could also try to ask for advice. Most of the time people love to give advice and share their opinions.

LEVERAGING EXISTING RESOURCES AND CONTACTS

We already have the resources: our network, our knowledge, and our language skills. You don't get these things overnight; you build them over many years. Most translators provide one-on-one service: you get the work and spend time working on each project, you hand in the project, and you get paid. Why not try to reach out to other professionals also selling to your target market? You can work with these other service providers, and also think of ways to repackage your combined knowledge and skills. For example, providing a podcast to help other translators market their business and get clients could be done for free, but it's likely that beginners wouldn't mind paying X dollars (or any other currency) for a service that helps them to get clients faster.

Here's another example: Let's say you know somebody who wants to learn Swedish. Many translators teach languages on the side, but what you can do differently is package these lessons into webinars or even PowerPoint slides. That way you can leverage your knowledge and you don't have to be there when you teach. You can give users a product that is already finished, and if they have questions, they can always come back to you for in-person support. Translators need to think from that efficient perspective and value their skills more.

From interview with Joy Mo [www.proz.com/profile/1180658], *a freelance translator and certified Mandarin/English Court Interpreter in BC, Canada.*

How can a freelance translator use negotiation skills when they are marketing translation services? When you have found a prospective client and told them that you can provide the type of service they might need, you must convince them that you are the right person for that job. It's not enough to tell them that you are the English to Swedish translator that they need. You must actually get the message across that you are an English to Swedish translator who can be trusted to do the work. Negotiation skills, while not directly related to marketing, are a way of making sure that you are conveying the right image. You have to present yourself professionally, as someone who is reliable, trustworthy and is going to meet deadlines. You also must convey that you are going to get the job done at the level of quality that they need.

Conveying a message of reliability and trustworthiness can be done while negotiating in writing or over the phone. If you are dealing with somebody by email, you have more time to consider exactly what you need to write and how to write it. Of course, you lose that human level of connection, but for someone who is not very experienced in negotiations, it may offer an opportunity to think carefully about what they want to say.

When you are talking with people on the phone, it is very important that you sound professional. That means not speaking too quickly, not rambling, addressing all the points that the client makes, and being very clear and to the point. If you can establish a connection with someone, if you can make them laugh, it will make a big difference in how you communicate with them and how the relationship proceeds from that point.

Dealing with an existing client will be the easiest negotiation you'll ever have. If you think about the price of anything, it's simply a reflection of the value people place on that product or service. The difference between a potential clients you haven't worked with and an existing client is that the potential client doesn't really know what value you offer, they can only guess. The existing client already knows your value, knows who you are and what you can do, and that's why they are working with you. An existing client is much easier, because they keep coming back to you. One of the tricks I use a lot is to increase my rates for new clients before I increase them for my regular clients. That means, if I come to an existing client a year down the line and say to them, "Well, we've been working together for three years now. It's been a great relationship. I've really enjoyed it and it seems that you have too. However, all this time my rates have been going up and I've been doing my very best to keep them at their current price level for you. Can we talk about how to bring them more in line with what I am charging now?" Posing this question against the backdrop that you are increasing rates for other clients is something most clients will be open to discussing.

HOW TO DEAL WITH DIFFICULT OR DEMANDING CLIENTS

Never take anything personally. This is something that most translators struggle with a lot. Clients who demand a very short deadline are not being ridiculous; it's more of an expression of something they need. They are not demanding speed because they are bad person, or because they want to oppress the translator. They are doing it as a way of saying, "Hey, I need this done quickly." Maybe they can't even use the translation if it's not done quickly. You just have to find a mutually acceptable outcome, even if that outcome is you turning down the job. That is still a mutually acceptable outcome, especially if you handle it with sensitivity.

If a client wants a lower rate (due to the economic situation, budget, volume, etc.), you have to decide whether the rate that they suggest is acceptable to you or not. If it's not, then there are two options: one **is to turn the job down, the other** is to say, "It's not acceptable and we have been working at a different rate. I understand your situation, but this is my rate. There is plenty of work going at that rate. So, let's talk about how we can find some middle ground." This solution is actually an important one that people sometimes forget.

Not everyone who contacts you, and not everyone who is currently your client, is necessarily a good client for you. You will shed clients as your business grows. Say no regularly and do it with pleasure. If you can't do something, be clear about it and know that people will respect you. Also, try to take charge of the conversation. The way to do that is to ask questions about the project, or about the client if you are dealing with them for the first time. Often, asking questions is a way to take charge of the conversation.

Finish conversations by summarizing your actions. It is a statement of who is in charge and who is in control of that conversation. Let's say you and your client are finishing a conversation, and they have told you what they need. You've told them that you can probably do the job, but you need them to send you the file to check. At the end of the conversation, you say, "OK, that's great. Thank you for your call. I'm going to wait for you to send me the file. Once I've received it, I'll analyze it, and get back to you as soon as possible with a quote and a suggested deadline."

Email requires a different approach, but you still want to address every point that the client makes. When your client sends you a massive stream of consciousness paragraph, with no hard returns, take it apart piece-by-piece and answer them back in bullet points. It will give both you and your client a structure for future correspondence. Make sure that you respond to everything and be as clear and deliberate as possible. Don't ramble. Don't put things in your message that are unrelated. Keep your language very professional.

NEGOTIATION MISTAKES TO AVOID

Some translators may feel limited in the choices they have when they are negotiating with a customer. For example, they may feel like they must either give an ultimatum, or give in to whatever their clients want to do. It creates a sense of powerlessness, which is inappropriate, because as a service provider, you have a lot of power and a lot of influence over what happens.

Probably the biggest mistake people make, not just in the translation industry but in general, is confusing negotiation skills with assertiveness. People think that you have to be assertive to be a good negotiator. Nothing could be further from the truth.

Being assertive annoys people more than anything else does. All you really need is a bit of clarity about your goals, rates, and objectives, and the confidence that you can do the job that is being discussed.

From interview with Konstantin Kisin
[www.proz.com/translator/82508], a bilingual Russian translator, working in the fields of economic, finance, politics, marketing and sports, as well as video game development.

Whatever it is that you love to do in life, sales can help you achieve it. Making a sale is all about converting a prospect into a client. Stage one is marketing and getting new prospects. Stage two is converting those prospects into actual sales or clients.

FIRST CONTACT

A prospect is someone who has either emailed you or contacted you in some way to express interest in your services. The first step is to pick up the phone and talk to them.

This is where a lot of people can get lost, because they will have the initial call, they will quote the document, and then things will die down after that.

MONITORING

The next stage of the sales process is monitoring. Having a good monitoring process could increase your sales by 50 to 100 percent. It consists of calling the client a few days after delivering a quote to see what they thought of it, and ask if they need any further information. Sometimes when prospects ask for a quote they don't always have a job at hand or, if they do, it might require some sort of approval from someone else in their company, their boss or their boss' boss. A length of time may pass between the initial contact and the point at which they can actually approve the job. The more you can keep in touch with the prospect during this period, without getting to the point of annoying them, the better. Use a combination of phone calls and reminder emails to maintain contact with the client.

The final step is to close the sale. This process is really about converting the person who is very interested, the person who has been talking to you all of this time, into a client. You may want to make them some kind of limited offer in order to encourage an immediate decision. It could be something along the lines of locking in a discounted price for a limited time only, or a request to confirm the business by such and such a date in order to ensure translator availability. I'm not a big fan of these high-pressure sales tactics, but I do think that prospects sometimes need to be helped to make a decision. Therefore, this final part of the sales process can be really important.

Be prepared to negotiate. Perhaps your prospective client has obtained other quotes that are 10% lower than yours. You might use that as an opportunity to talk about the reasons why they should go with you or your company. It's always valuable to point out the advantages you can offer in terms of who you've worked with before, how you've done similar jobs and so on. And if you are prepared to drop your quote by 5%, even though you would still be the most expensive bidder, you might then become the more attractive option. If you realize that you've lost the client, try to speak to them and ask them why they decided to go with someone else. Most of the time they won't answer, but roughly 25-30% of the time they do share really useful information.

The "Seven Points of Contact" theory suggests that you have to have seven contacts with a client (whether it's an email, a phone call, or something else) before they will actually do the deal with you. If you've been in constant contact with these people, they already know and like you, and maybe they trust you and are ready to go ahead. The 5% difference in price isn't going to be that relevant at the end of the day.

Be persistent. Some people find it difficult to do so, but it is a very important part of the sales process. You should continue until you get a yes or a no out of the person to whom you are pitching.

Focus on continued learning. Read a lot of books about sales. Translation books are excellent, but I think from time to time it's important to read pure sales books, or books about sales in other industries. Also, talk and interact with salespeople. If you've got any friends or family members or contacts who are salespeople, ask if you can have a cup of coffee with them and find out how they sell to people. You will find that most salespeople have a lot in common across industries, so read books and learn from salespeople.

From interview with Paul Urwin *[www.100percentlanguages.com], a languages entrepreneur, speaker, coach, digital author and CEO of 100% Languages.*

CHAPTER 3 – MARKETING

Marketing is about knowing yourself and the unique and special qualities you have to offer potential clients. Effective marketing strategies are not only essential for growing your client base, but also for attracting better-paying clients, or those who can offer the kinds of assignments that play to your strengths and preferences. In this chapter, I've collected some great ideas about marketing from established international translators. Their practical advice is part of my podcast Marketing Tips for Translators — find out more about these translation professionals at the end of each section.

What is branding and how do we do it well? A brand is something that usually evokes trust. The basic concept is that of an established entity, usually suggested by a logo, brand name or some other feature.

People will buy into the perceived value of what you can present to them. As a freelancer you will decide whether you want to be a company, or be represented by an agent, or maybe work with a group of colleagues. It will depend on what sort of entity you want to be. It all comes down to the image you are thinking about conveying to others.

HOW TO START BRANDING

Figure out what it is about yourself that you want to market and why. Then, concentrate on the how. You can do this by first identifying your clients and prospects. If you have recently graduated from college and are just starting out, you can start fresh and build something from the beginning with a logo or name. Get a page, a profile, or a very simple website. Then you can start to make yourself visible as a persona, as a personal brand. A more serious corporate identity can come later. Find out what you like about your line of work. As soon as you have clearer ideas or gain some specialization, you can start thinking about branding. Plan to commit to your brand for life.

An experienced translator can simply polish what they already have. If they have an existing page or profile, it may be outdated and due for a refresh. Most online sites are typically refreshed every two months.

- Sometimes, you may have a great idea but no way to put it into practice. Collaborating with a designer can help if you don't personally have those creative skills.

- Remember that color palettes work differently in print than in real life. Be careful about using obsolete techniques or styles (for example sites that use Adobe Flash animation and similar).

- Avoid putting too much information on a page, or you may crowd or unbalance your logo, making it difficult to understand. Immediate clarity and understanding is important when it comes to logos – the viewer must immediately associate it with something.

From interview with Valeria Aliperta
[www.rainylondontranslations.com], a UK-based professional conference interpreter and translator, and founder of Rainy London Translations.

Within the marketing industry we can distinguish between two types of marketing strategies: B2B (business to business) or B2C (business to customer). B2B marketing is promotions or sales that take place between two companies or businesses. B2C marketing implies selling services or products to a consumer rather than to a business. The reason these two strategies are so different is that consumers and businesses behave differently. Customers' decisions are more emotional and can be influenced by the flavor or story behind the brand, or the fact that they can get involved with the brand history or become part of an associated community. When it comes to business, decisions are based on a more rational decision-making process. How much is it going to cost? What are the benefits? Why should I work with another business? It is important for us to understand the differences, and to apply that understanding to everything from the creation of a website to the way we use social media or the way we write resumes or emails.

HOW TO REACH OTHER BUSINESSES WITH OUR MARKETING MESSAGE

We need to be rational and demonstrate potential profitability in our marketing messages to companies. Messages should be focused on imagining what a business goes through when it is looking online for a translation service. How can we help them? Aside from the identity or creative flavor suggested by our brand, what services can we provide? Clients want to know what they are paying for, and where their money is going. This is not like a job interview; this is a business-to-business relationship, so you are focusing on the actual benefits your translation services will bring to the business with which you are working. Will they increase sales, for instance? Will they send a message to new markets so your client will find partners and trade with your country?

B2B marketing is a process, and the first step in that process is generating leads. Those leads should also generate other leads. Catching the attention of a business is really complicated – they may receive thousands of emails daily, and are constantly bombarded by advertising or account marketing. You need to become visible in order to get their attention. You could use social media, or create a website and a blog, for example, and try to engage with them rather than simply bombard them with advertising. More specifically, in the case of translation businesses using websites, for example, we need to work on search engine optimization (SEO), which is very important if you want people to immediately see the benefits of using your services.

THE FIVE MOST IMPORTANT TIPS WHEN MARKETING TO BUSINESSES

1. Always do market research before committing to any kind of marketing activity. Creating materials can cost you money, and if they are not effective, you are never going to use them again.

2. Be specific, find your target market and then do research to try to understand the language these businesses are using. What they are talking about? What do they need?

3. Consider using social media to get in touch with potential clients. It is just one of the many effective tools available.

4. Target companies within a very specific field or niche – it does not matter how obscure or specialized they are.

5. When doing research, start with Google and a general set of keywords that use the name of the company and the type of product the company is producing, then look deeper. Not all companies are online, and some have websites that are not clear about what they do. It may take some time to gather all the information.

HOW TO MARKET YOUR TRANSLATION SERVICES TO DIRECT CLIENTS YOU CANNOT MEET

What happens if you can't go to an industry conference to connect with potential clients? One of the things you can do to reach out to potential clients is to advertise in trade journals. Have your ads designed by a graphic designer to ensure they look sharp and professional. You might include the name of your company, your logo (again prepared by a graphic designer) and a really simple bullet list of your articles, marketing brochures, name and website. It can be a very simple, straightforward ad.

Internal referrals are another method. The key here is to do excellent work. If the client is happy and they are willing to say so, ask them for an endorsement for your website. And then let them know that you're available for other work.

WARM EMAIL PROSPECTING

Identify your ideal client and the target company that could use your services. Find contact information by doing a web search. Keep an eye out for news or announcements concerning the company. Once you have an item of news, such as a listing about the company going public on a stock exchange, or something about launching a new product, use that news as an excuse to contact the potential client. Tell them who you are, and how you could help grow their company, or help by translating documents and reaching out to clients. Then, ask for a meeting or to be introduced to a certain person within the company.

STEALTH MARKETING

Stealth marketing can be subtle. It can be as basic as the free sample idea: in return for a free registration to the next big industry conference, offer to do some work for free. You'll get to attend a conference, and your work constitutes free advertising for your services straight to your target market.

Offer to do a short talk about translation at a meeting just to further raise your profile. As people who go to industry conferences may have noticed, industry people often don't really understand the process of translation, or what's really needed. Offer an educational session to raise awareness.

MISTAKES WHEN MARKETING TO DIRECT CLIENTS

One mistake is not setting aside enough time every week or month for marketing and to let potential clients know about your services. You have to find a way to stay in touch with prospective clients, even if you don't get work from them right away. Find some way to get in touch with them every few months, just so they will remember you.

From interview with Joanne Archambault [www.traduction-ortho.com], *an ATA-certified French to English translator specializing in pharmaceutical and orthopedics industry documents.*

We all know that we should have a marketing plan for our small business or freelance translation service, but how do we create one that relates specifically to our industry? Let's look at the elements of a good marketing plan – the objective, the products and services you are dealing with, how to find your unique selling points, and how to segment your market, analyze competition, and find the best prospects that fit you.

ANALYSIS

The starting point is always analysis. You need to know where you stand right now. For example, are you a new freelance translator, or an experienced one? Who are your customers today, and who are your competitors? What differentiates you from your competitors? The analysis doesn't have to be difficult. You can just sit down and answer the following questions to create a strong foundation on which to build a marketing plan:

- What do you want to achieve? You should have a clear understanding of your goals. For example, do you want to move from being a part-time translator to full-time? Do you want better clients or higher pay? Do you want to become known for your expertise? Do you want to add more clients to an existing roster? Do you want to develop a new specialization, for example? Choose one of these goals to provide focus for your plan.

- What is your marketing niche? Answering this will help you focus on target clients, because you can't market to all of them. For example, are you a French into English translator and do you want to work with lawyers? If so, then that's your niche.

- Who are your customers today, and who are your ideal future customers? Are they translation companies? Are they

87

localization companies, or are they individual clients? Are they mostly located in the United States, or in Europe? In which industry are they mostly working?

- Who are your competitors? Do you consider translation companies or agencies your competitors, or are there other freelance translators that you consider to be your competitors? Where are they located? It's good to know as much as possible about the competition in order to determine what makes you unique. Remember that competition is not a war, and you can start collaborating with competitors instead of competing with them.

- What are your unique selling points? For example, are you the only translator in your niche, in your city, state or region? Does your time zone work to your advantage? What about your availability, your speed, or the tools you know how to use? Does your professional background or education make you different? For example, do you have a PhD in medical research?

These are the five questions to ask yourself while building an analysis-based foundation. From here you can start assembling the basic elements of a marketing plan.

OBJECTIVES

Look at objectives and long-term goals. Where do you want to be in five years? Break it down into annual or monthly goals. When you do this, you can define the main purpose of your marketing plan. For example, maybe you want to increase sales by 25% within a few years, or maybe your goal is to translate 1.5 million words for ten of your ideal clients within a year. Once you know your objectives, break them down into specific and strategic marketing goals. Define your ideal clients or prospects. What are their needs? Where are they located? What are their demographics? Where can you find them and how can you find them?

Another element of any good marketing plan is how to attract and win your ideal clients. You can focus on sending direct mail to prospects, or you can focus on filling out online applications through translation agencies and registering in forums. You can join a new translation association, or you can call people and follow up on leads.

You should also define how to work on retaining your clients. Customer care is one of your most important marketing tools. Figure out how to keep the clients you have, which ones you like best, and what makes them desirable. Try to find more clients like them.

You should then identify your communication goals. What do you want to achieve with your marketing? Do you want to create or reinforce positive opinions about yourself? Do you want to change negative opinions? What is your goal? Do you just want to encourage people to get to know you? Do you want them to get to know you for your expertise, or for some other quality?

Another important aspect of a marketing plan is your financial goals. How much do you want to earn and how much do you want to work? This is something you need to balance. For example, do you just want to remain confident in your abilities and not lower your rates? Do you want to convince your prospects that you offer something unique and are worth the higher price? In order to establish financial goals, you need to know where you are today. Track your finances by looking at your annual income for the past three years, and decide what you want it to be in the next three. Which client generates the most income or how many clients generate the most income? Of course, you must define your expenses as well.

PRODUCTS AND SERVICES OFFERED

Identify your products or services, but also define them more specifically. Do you only do translation, or do you also do proofreading, editing, copywriting or desktop publishing? How are these services different from those offered by other translators? For example, do you work in a unique or uncommon language combination? Do you have extensive professional and educational marketing experience? Just remember to define what your service is, know it by heart, and be able to describe what differentiates it from others. Remember that your target market might be different from the one you have now. Perhaps you want to find more direct clients instead of translation companies, or perhaps you want to focus more on a specific country or industry, or on a totally new market.

BUDGET

As freelance translators, we are pretty used to starting and maintaining a business without any big investments. Marketing doesn't have to be expensive, but it is beneficial to decide how much money you are willing and able to put into marketing before you get started. Remember that marketing is a worthy investment.

Build a database of your current customers and add as much information about them as you can. For example, how long have you been working for them? How many and what types of projects have you done for them? What are their payment practices and how big are they? Build on this database and keep in touch with current clients. It's helpful to use a content management system or a customer relationship management system. Free or very affordable ones exist for downloading, but simple Excel sheets or even your bookkeeping software might also work.

Now that you have identified your existing customers and your prospective or ideal clients based on the market research, demonstrate that you know the customer and can solve problems for them. When you market to direct clients, it's very important to customize each letter to each customer. Don't forget to also network with prospects online through social platforms and industry conferences.

MARKETING MATERIALS

When you create your marketing material, or write your letter to a prospective agency or client, try to answer these questions:

- Why should they hire you?

- How can you help make this company successful?

- What value can you provide, and can you explain how the ideal client's bottom line will be affected? For example, if they don't have a translated website, how will their bottom line be affected if they don't translate it, and what could happen if you help them with translating it?

An important part of your marketing plan should be to create a multilingual website, or a website in the language that your target clients use. A website can be the hub for all your marketing efforts; it's where you can show off your message and target it to your clients' needs.

Make yourself more visible and demonstrate your expertise by writing articles to publications related to either the translation or the interpreting industry. You can also try to write an article for your target client's industry publication and get yourself known in that community.

You can network both online and offline. Online you can network with fellow translators, or you can focus on your prospects by having a profile on LinkedIn. You can also use Facebook and Twitter. A blog is also good, but if you don't have one, you can still participate in others' translation blogs.

Ask for referrals and recommendations from your existing clients. Get involved in your local translation chapter or national translation associations. All of this activity will build your presence in the industry and in the market.

One of the most important, yet most underused, features in a marketing plan is tracking and following up. For example, do you track your income, the number of clients you have, the number of visitors to your website, and the number of recurring jobs from existing clients? When a new client contacts you, asking where they heard about you is good standard practice. Research shows that 80% of marketing goes to waste (it's the so-called 80/20 principle), so you had better identify the 20% that is working.

If you send direct mail to prospects, it's very important to follow up within a week or two. Send another email, or send another letter, or call. Ask if they have any questions and if they're interested, or if they have no immediate need for your services – you can always try again in four to six months. Just keep yourself on their radar. Also, track how many customers you had before and after you implemented the marketing plan. How has your online presence increased? For example, how many people have viewed your materials online? How many are calling or writing you back? Make use of tools such as Google Analytics, which is free. Many other tools for tracking online statistics exist as well.

Does all this seem overwhelming? It doesn't have to be. Several examples of one-page marketing plans are available online (search for "one-page marketing plan"), and that may be all you need to get started. Set your goals and make a to-do list (write down the steps, and try to follow them), and use your research to get you to the point at which you want to be.

*From solo episode with **Tess Whitty***
[www.marketingtipsfortranslators.com/episode-020-elements-marketing-plan-translators]

CREATING "MARKETING PERSONAS" FOR YOUR FREELANCE TRANSLATION BUSINESS

Marketing personas are profiles of your customers and prospects that contain important information. They usually take the shape of a fictional character that embodies the characteristics of your target audience, including details about their employment. For example, a marketing profile could include a character's salary, or their project volumes, or the kind of languages they use, but could also include general information about their customer behavior.

Break your target audience down into smaller groups with similar characteristics in order to understand what might or might not click with them when doing marketing activities. A smaller group from the broader audience can then be distilled into a persona or avatar. While they are generally anonymous and constructed out of your "imagination", some companies do give names to marketing personas. The idea is to narrow down your target customer base so that you can speak to them specifically, rather than always speaking to an undefined audience. This allows you to sound more personal in your communications.

One of the disadvantages for freelancers is inadequate budget or time to go deeper into market research. It is a bit of work to narrow down what a customer wants and needs, but it is not impossible. And, it can definitely pay off.

USING MARKETING PERSONAS FOR IMPROVED MARKETING

Personas can help you spot opportunities to meet prospects in the real world. This is really underrated, because meeting people can be a vital step in the marketing process. You meet a person and make contact; that person may not need you, but may know someone who does, and they will move fast if you are in the right environment. You can use your marketing persona as a tool to select events or conferences you want to attend. For example, if you wanted to make contact with medical translation clients, don't go to a general conference or a translation event; go to a medical conference. You have to go where the customer is.

QUESTIONS TO ASK WHEN DEVELOPING MARKETING PERSONAS

- It can be helpful to know what kinds of communication the customer has already done in terms of their marketing. Go to their website and look at their materials to understand the style and tone of voice they use. Who is this customer as a businessperson? Is he a project manager or a small business owner? While we are really attuned to our own jargon, direct customers aren't, so you can't just go to a business owner and talk about tools he doesn't know about – it's a waste of time.

- Ask what services your customer generally requests. Identifying the types of services they have used most often in the past may provide new opportunities for development.

- How does the project manager make his or her decision to purchase? Does he need something quick and dirty? Do they have to fix a huge mistake, or are they looking for something with more quality and consistency? Are they very budget-oriented, and do they have time constraints? Would they typically plan in advance for a translation?

94

- Who makes the decision when it comes to paying your bill? When you talk directly to a business owner, he may be the one in charge, but if you talk to a company, they may have an accounting department or maybe a budget and planning department. Your quote doesn't necessarily end up with the project manager; he may pass it on to someone else.

- In terms of industry knowledge, are there any common pressures that can make a customer more difficult, or easier, to work with? Also, what kind of project specifications do they usually request? If you can handle only a limited number of file types, for example, could it be a barrier to them buying your services if you can't fit their requirements?

- Which elements of your products or services will the client actually value? Some value communication – they may already have a history of responding to you online. Other clients may be very independent and not enjoy being asked too many questions.

- Another very important question to ask is how the company would use your products or services. Do you need to translate for internal use only, or will your work be put online? If the latter is the case, you will need to pay attention to web writing rules. Does your client's brochure need to go to a small number of local companies, or is it for a nationwide campaign? What will your copy be doing when it is ready to go out into the world?

- What are your client's interests outside of work or the office, and what are their lifestyles like? When a person is very conservative, or likes very traditional things, you can't be too dynamic or revolutionary in your conversations.

From interview with Alessandra Martelli [*www.mtmtranslations.com*], *a translator, copywriter and trainer based in Turin, Italy.*

Warm email prospecting could also be called "artisanal prospecting," because it requires emails that are handcrafted. What you are trying to do is to create a very short and relevant custom email message to a specific individual. When they open it and start reading, they should have no doubt that it was written just for them. This is the opposite of a mass email broadcast. You are inviting someone to connect with you to see if you have a reason to talk further. Warm email prospecting is warm because you are sending a personalized message to an individual with whom you want to do business.

We live in an automated society; we are used to copying and pasting and to efficiency – we strive for that. However, warm email prospecting is one of those activities with which you must take your time; it's not about quantity, it's about quality. It may take an hour to send out one email because of the necessary research and the care you need to take in crafting it. But you are better off sending a couple of warm emails a week than you are sending two hundred emails a week that are copied and pasted. Don't blindly go down a list of people. For everyone you send an email, there must be a very strategic reason for reaching out to them. Perhaps you see a potential match between your services, offerings, or values and their organization. The more targeted you are, the higher your response rate will be.

In today's crowded inbox world, most of us want those types of messages. When everything else we are getting is mass marketed emails, or office communications on which everyone is being copied, to get something from someone new that was written specifically for you, that is relevant, short and to the point, is such a refreshing change. This is what makes warm prospecting so effective.

THE DIFFERENCE FROM SENDING A REGULAR SALES LETTER OR EMAIL

A direct mail piece has its place in a marketing strategy, but with these, everyone gets the same message. As a recipient, you automatically know this has been written to ten thousand other people. You know that it is advertising and marketing and, depending on where you might be in terms of your business needs and the details of the offer, you might or might not respond. Regular mail messages can be worthwhile and very effective when done well, but you must resist the temptation to mass-create these things and get them out there. The goal here is not efficiency; the goal is personalization and relevance. Acknowledge the person you are addressing and make it clear that this message is just for them.

PAY ATTENTION TO THE SUBJECT LINE

When receiving an email, we sometimes look only at the subject line, so meaningful connection should be part of your subject line. Let's say that you notice an organization has posted a lot of white papers on its site, and you happen to be good at translating white papers. The subject line could read "Translating your white papers." As a marketing director, that alone would get your attention, because you have been posting a lot of white papers on your site. You do not know the sender of the message; maybe it's a prospect, a partner, whoever, but the subject line will probably get you to open the email.

Do not give away too much in the subject line. It should not necessarily be thorough and complete; rather it should tease the prospect enough to want to open the email. Give them only enough to show them it is relevant to their business and that they should open the email.

Three strategies for implementing warm email prospecting are extremely effective: routine prospecting, ad hoc prospecting and hot list prospecting.

The most realistic way to implement **routine prospecting** is to carve out some time every week to read industry or trade journals and publications, magazines that are important for your target markets (or the equivalent websites or online publications). Start thinking about using research as a prospecting tool and schedule some time every week to read through materials. The fact that someone is expanding, moving, seems to be getting a lot of press, or is on a top fifty list for companies or products to watch – these could all become potential ideas for connecting.

Come up with at least two or three potential targets and dig into their websites. Start with a bit of general research and see if you can uncover more. Sometimes a news announcement or article will give you enough to proceed. Then, craft emails to the individuals you've discovered. This is considered routine prospecting because you are actually scheduling time every week, or every other week, to go through publications and find opportunities.

Ad hoc prospecting is something for which you do not even have to plan. It is set in motion when you get an industry newsletter or a newsletter from one of your target industries that contains an announcement or story that triggers an idea.

Hot list prospecting involves creating a list of ten to twenty dream clients, clients that you would love to work for at some point in your career, but who are not current clients. Dig a little into the background of each one and see if you can find connections or subjects about which you can approach them. Because this is a list of ten or twenty, you are not going to be able to do this in a single afternoon. This is a longer-term effort, the kind on which you will have to spend more time. Because they are dream clients, you should be willing to invest this kind of time and send multiple emails over the course of a year, or even two years. Send them warm emails occasionally on different topics about what you are doing that you think would interest them.

There are several strategies for prospecting, and most of them involve detective work. Some people reading this will want to automate this work, or buy or rent a list. That would be starting off the wrong way. You want to look for needs, possibilities and potential opportunities first, and then dig deep. You might use LinkedIn to find the name of an individual and their title. LinkedIn has a wonderful advanced search feature, and you can set criteria for the company, department and so forth. Sort through the results and determine which people would be the most appropriate to approach.

You could also use Google to search for a person's name and email address. Google has some advanced search features that allow you to search for very specific terms. What you are looking for are mentions of this person, their name and email address somewhere out there on the Web.

If you do not find their email address on LinkedIn or Google, 80% to 90% of the time you can find it with this next tool. It's a Salesforce product that used to be called Jigsaw. Now it is called Data.com Connect [www.connect.data.com]. Essentially, this is a database containing the contact information for tens of millions of people. You do not even have to sign up for it; simply punch in someone's name and it will give you most of their information, except for a direct phone number and email address. However, they will tell you if they have those, and you can do one of two things at that point: trade some of the contact information in your own address book to get points, which you can then use to buy that contact, or you can buy one of their plans. It costs about $250 a year and you get several hundred prospect names based on the number of points you purchase.

END WITH A CALL TO ACTION

Include a call to action asking to connect, and provide your contact details. You want to keep things brief – 125 words or less. The shorter the better, and the higher the chances that someone will actually read it.

LEAD NURTURING

Lead nurturing is about staying in touch with prospects that may not be a good fit today, usually because of bad timing. Perhaps they do sometimes hire translators, but right now they don't have anything for you. Across virtually every industry you will find that people forget about those kinds of leads. Lead nurturing is about staying in touch with those people in a value-added way. Think about sending them the occasional article or handwritten note, or a link to a case study, and describe how you helped a similar client solve a particular challenge. Space your messages so you don't seem like a pest. You want to stay at the top of their mind right up to the moment they are ready to hire you. The moment they need a translator, you want to be the first person they recall.

*From interview with **Ed Gandia** [www.b2blauncher.com], founder of High-Income Business Writing and co-author of the bestselling and award-winning book, The Wealthy Freelancer.*

Becoming a literary translator is not an easy undertaking. It's very difficult to get any sort of translation work published. However, it is extremely rewarding and there are many ways of going about it. To begin with, you have to know who has published what. What are the genres that require translation? Which publishers deal in translation? What is the market like? What will it bear? How do you write a query letter to propose or pitch a project to a publishing house, or an editor, or an author? You must know almost as much about publishing and writing as you do about translation.

START WITH CONTACTING SMALLER PUBLISHERS

Contacting big publishers is probably going to be a waste of your time. They are very unlikely to respond to unsolicited emails and CVs. With smaller publishers, you can make that personal connection and find precisely the right editor to approach.

AND AUTHORS

99% of the time authors are going to be thrilled that you wrote to them to say you would like to translate their work. They'll often work with you to try to make it happen, give you permission to translate and publish their work. Connecting with people doesn't have to occur in person, but try to make a real connection. Find that one thing that you have in common. Offer something that they may not even know they wanted.

Referrals mean a lot. Publishers will have their favorite translators, but if that translator is busy, or a language is required with which the publisher has never worked, they'll probably find a new translator by asking around. That's when making your name known and connecting with authors and editors and publishers can pay off.

CREATE A PORTFOLIO

Your portfolio should be like any other artist's portfolio – with samples of your published work that are added over time. It can also showcase pieces you've translated that you have permission for and hope will be published. Your portfolio provides proof of what you're able to do as a literary translator. You should also have a literary CV that summarizes your history in this area. As you know, CVs should be specific to whomever you're sending them. A literary CV has a different focus than the CV you would send to an agency or a private client. It's going to hone in and focus on your publishing credits (if you have any), and any writing experience that you might have, including your own writing, and whether or not it has been published. This type of CV is much more compact, usually only about one page long, and is tailored to highlight your writing and publishing skills.

From interview with Lisa Carter [www.intralingo.com], a
Spanish/English translator and consultant who runs a boutique service in
Canada called Intralingo.

CHAPTER 4 – PRODUCTIVITY

Productivity is always a concern for the self-employed and small business owner. It's also something that can be continually improved and maximized. Contemporary business culture supplies a steady stream of tips, advice and tools to boost daily productivity. Everyone will find different things helpful, but the underlying need to get the most out of each working day is universally important. I've compiled some of my own favorite productivity strategies in this chapter, along with tips from experts I've interviewed for my podcast, <u>Marketing Tips for Translators</u> — find out more about these translation professionals at the end of each section.

TIME MANAGEMENT AND FINDING BALANCE

Being a freelance translator is both rewarding and challenging. One of the biggest challenges is managing our time so we don't end up working around the clock, or burning out. If we are constantly working, we also lack time to market our services to "better" clients.

JUGGLING WORK AND LIFE

Clients can now contact you at all times because of smartphones. Everyone has constant access to the Internet. Clients will assume no matter the time of day, you're going to be available to respond to them, or at least receive their messages. You may work with overseas clients so there may also be a time zone issue. You may be nine hours away and you'll have to be able to respond by 9:00 am your time, otherwise the client will have left for the day.

When you work at home, people assume you're just baking cookies all day long. And, in fact, it's very difficult to keep family and work tasks separate.

Often the reason we don't make regular business hours and stick to them is because we are fearful. We have tons of fear that if we don't respond to everything immediately we're going to lose clients. We won't be available when the message arrives and that will be the end of the world. Fear is what really keeps us from setting out exactly what it is we want to achieve, how we want to work, and pursuing it.

It's vital to take time off for yourself to avoid burnout. A lot of people will quit a job, thinking that its way too much work. But any kind of job involves time management, and if you don't learn crucial time management skills and develop discipline around them, you're just going to burn out at the next job.

104

An information survey presented at an ATA conference in recent years asked about the challenges of time management. A majority of respondents, about 64%, said the biggest challenge was procrastinating. Just over half complained about being easily distracted. Just under half (44%) said they couldn't say no to anything. Some (about 42%) said responsibilities outside of work had a huge impact on how they managed their time. About one-quarter felt they had taken on too much work, or they had trouble prioritizing. And about 16% complained about feeling overwhelmed. Ten percent felt they didn't have a good place to work, and that this was impacting their ability to manage their time.

Another part of this survey asked about repercussions. We asked people the results of these challenges; many responded by saying that they worked late at night, or started early in the morning to get everything done. About 64% said they don't have enough time for non-work interests. About that same proportion felt that they were stressed about their work-life balance. Half of those surveyed felt very stressed about work. Half the respondents felt that they were finishing projects at the very last minute. Twenty percent felt that they were missing family events, forgetting deadlines, and asking for extensions. Fortunately, only 12% said that they were actually missing deadlines, a fairly low percentage.

DISTRACTIONS

One of the main problems cited by survey respondents was being easily distracted. Here's how to deal with some of the most common distraction culprits:

- Email is a huge distraction. Get a good junk filter, because junk mail can be deceiving. Sometimes you can't figure out if it's junk mail or not, and that's wasting your time. Create subfolders or, if you're working with Google's Gmail, work with the labels feature that allows you to separate personal mail from work mail.

- Microsoft Outlook is a powerful tool that allows you to look for mail from specific people that you designate, or specific words in the subject line, or words within the body of the text. You can create different folders and tell Outlook to, for example, put ATA-related messages in the ATA folder. If an email comes from a particular client, put it in an urgent request folder and add a reminder to let you know that this needs to be addressed.

- All those posts and notifications on Facebook or LinkedIn can go into a separate folder for you to review when you have time. Set a time to check your email each day. You don't need to check it every 15 minutes; you can check it every 30 minutes, or every hour, and some people even go a little longer than that. However, don't let it go too long. You don't want a lot of messages to which you haven't replied piling up to the point that clients start calling you.

- If your email message needs to be longer than five lines, call the person. Don't waste time trying to type a response, because people don't read lengthy emails. They skim. Project managers, in particular, have no time. They are probably juggling four or five projects at the same time, so reply briefly. If you feel you need to send a longer reply, give them a call.

- If you want to receive fewer emails, send fewer emails. Think before you copy everybody on everything. As for incoming emails, the bottom line is to either respond, delete, or mark the message as unread to deal with later. If you need to respond immediately, do it. If you can respond later, fine. Otherwise delete the thing.

TACKLING PROCRASTINATION

- Look for the kind of work that you enjoy, and take on those projects — you will find yourself procrastinating less. If you're interested in a particular type of translation, or if you like working for a particular client, seek out those jobs. Don't just take on everything that lands in your inbox on a first-come, first-serve basis. If the job turns out to be a disaster, you'll be miserable. If you're working on something you like, with a client you like, then it's easy not to procrastinate.

- Find somebody who can help you with marketing. Find somebody who can help you with billing. Find somebody who can help you with family tasks, or all the other things that you have to do. Use a calendar to visualize your time so when a client calls you and you agree to do a job, you can be sure you don't have another big project due at the same time. Keep a big monthly calendar in front of the computer and write everything on it so you can see how much time is actually available to do different activities.

- Take 15 minutes each day, or an hour or so on the weekend before the work week starts, and create a list of things that you want to accomplish within the week. Categorize them as A, B or C. Then, focus on the A's, of which you shouldn't have too many. Once you get the A's done, work on the B's and then the C's. I always find it helps to review the day's plan in the morning. Focus on what you have to do, and then on what you would like to do — you might find that there isn't that much that you absolutely have to do right away. You'll feel like the

107

pressure is off, which can help you focus and get the A items done, and then move on to the next item.

- Some people get their energy late at night. Adjust your schedule so that you are doing the most difficult tasks at those times of the day when you have a lot of energy. Then do your random invoicing, cleaning or other kinds of catching-up tasks at those times when you don't have as much energy. Figure out whether you're a morning person, afternoon person, or a late-night person and work accordingly. It will help you to stop procrastinating.

WORKSPACE

Your work area or office should be a fun place to hang out. If you're working long hours in a place that you don't like, in somebody's closet, or working at a tiny table that's not the right height, you're going to hate your job and not last long doing it. Add some nice furnishings and some pictures to your work area, and give yourself some inspiration. Find a place that is relatively quiet and dedicate that space so that when you leave it and close the door, you leave work. If it's a different part of the house, that's even better, because then it doesn't feel like your workspace is crowding your personal life.

*From an interview with **David Rumsey***
[www.northcountrytranslation.com], a translator from the Scandinavian languages into English at North Country Translation who specializes in technical, medical and commercial documentation.

There are nine basic principles for improving the way you work. The first one is called Live on Purpose, and it relates to knowing why you are doing whatever you are doing at any given moment. Two is to stop procrastinating. Three is to master your technology. Four is to beat distractions. Five is to stay organized. Six is to stop wasting time. Seven is to stay optimized. Eight is to build stronger relationships. And nine is to use leverage.

FIND A PROCRASTINATION BUDDY

The single best way I know to stop procrastinating is to find a procrastination buddy. If you are a freelancer, and are part of a community of freelance translators, find a buddy and agree that every day you will call each other at 10:00 am for mutual support about something each of you has been procrastinating.

Another way is to sign up for Do-it-days [www.DoitDays.com], it's free of charge. If you join the mailing list, you'll get an alert when one is coming up. The basic idea is simple: you get twelve people together, make a conference call at the top of every hour, and each person says what they've been doing and what they are planning to do next in two sentences or less. You go around all twelve people, and, once you are done, you hang up, go do the thing you've committed to and check back after an hour. It is a very simple format and, for a variety of reasons, it turns out to be very powerful in getting you to stop procrastinating. You will never have as productive a day as you do on a do it day. There are number of reasons for that, not the least of which is you have eleven other people cheering you on and waiting to hear how you did, and you do not want to let them down.

Connect with your procrastination buddy and work on anything you have been putting off. Then, if anything remains, sign up for a do it day and do it.

There is another brilliantly simple idea (created by a man named Mark Forrester in a book called *Get Everything Done and Still have Time to Play*) in which you make a list of the things you have been procrastinating. Choose four or five, write them down on a piece of paper, and draw three empty columns next to each one. Use graph paper so the columns are there automatically. You label the first column five minutes, the next column ten minutes and the third column fifteen minutes. Then you get out a timer and set it for five minutes, work on what's in the first column for five minutes, and then you put a check in the five column. Immediately work on the second task for five minutes, then the third task, then the fourth task, then the fifth task.

You give yourself a five-minute break, come back and do each one for ten minutes, and put a check in the ten column. Then, repeat the process for the fifteen minute column. You will be amazed at how the procrastination drops away and you begin to really get the work done.

Procrastination is not about whether or not you like the work, but what procrastination really is remains a mystery. Everyone procrastinates. We even procrastinate on the activities that we really want to do.

We tend to give urgent things higher priority than the things we love if those things are not urgent, which is probably a good thing for survival. I am not aware of any convenient way to set up my business so I only do the work I love. I need things like insurance, I have rent that needs to be paid, and taxes to file, and so on. I do not love any of those things, but if I do not do them I would live in the street, and I love that idea even less.

This concept is fairly simple. Let's say your goal is to write a book, and that book is going to be two hundred pages long, and you have ten months to do it. That means you have to write 20 pages a month, or one page a day if you assume there are 20 workdays in a month. All of a sudden, you can visualize how this project might be achieved. Take your major project, decide the time frame, and then just do the division to figure out the baby steps you need to do every day that will add up to a completed project within the chosen timeline. That becomes your daily action pack: the minimum number of steps you take on all of your important projects every day. Reviewing it should be the first thing you do when you start work in the morning. If your daily action pack is to write one page of your book, do that, but also call two prospective clients and clean your desk for five minutes. If you do each of these things every day, you will eventually finish your book, build a business, and clean your entire office. Do these things first and you will essentially be done for the day, because you will know that you will eventually reach your goals. Any other tasks you tackle that day are extra, and they can be any kind of work you want to do.

Setting a daily action pack to write six pages for your novel and call 400 prospects is not realistic. I know we are living in a culture in which everyone wants to believe they can do everything. The single most common question about productivity people wanting to know how they can do 26 hours of work in 24 hours. The answer is that you cannot. The key to the daily action pack is to break down your goals into as many small daily pieces as possible because you need to leave lots of room within your schedule to deal with the unexpected, to recharge and so on. If you really do work on your action pack every single day, you will make steady and constant progress, and eventually you will reach your goals. You will do it with the sum of lots of little steps.

CREATING FOCUS

Distractions are the result of a lack of discipline. If you work from home, have a dedicated area where you do your work and position your computer across the room, so it's not the only thing you look at when you are sitting at your desk. Shut down your web browser, cancel your Facebook account and turn off your email except during defined times.

These magical solutions will turn your computer into a focus device, rather than the distraction device they are engineered to be. Your job may require using a computer, but it's your choice whether or not to use it for distractions.

Email is one of the biggest of those distractions. You need to decide when you are going to check it. If you have real trouble getting sucked into email, designate a couple times a day, perhaps at the beginning and the end. Call an accountability buddy and go through your inboxes together. Stop after half an hour. Processing email does not mean acting on or responding to all the emails; it simply means going through your emails and turning them into to-do items. They then become a series of discrete tasks, which feels much easier to handle than the open-ended notion of processing email. For a half hour go through email with your buddy, turn messages into to-do items, and wrap it up at the end of the half hour.

ORGANIZING YOUR BRAIN

Getting organized is as much about organizing your brain as it is about organizing your workspace or office. People believe in multi-tasking, but according to the most recent research, too much multi-tasking turns your brain to jelly. It degrades your cognitive functioning, and it makes it very difficult to determine whether or not you are doing a good job. People who multi-task a lot believe they are doing a good job. But every piece of objective evidence in any study of multi-tasking shows that the more you do it, the less productive you are and the worse the quality of your results.

It helps to divide your days into a focus day, an administration day or a spirit day. On a focus day you do nothing other than really focused work; you are doing the tasks that add the highest value to your work. An administration day is when you do all the things that must get done but that do not directly add value to your business; for example, filling out expense reports, invoicing, calling people back about unimportant things, hiring subcontractors, etc.

Spirit days are days where you do not think about work at all, or if you do, just jot ideas in a notebook and continue enjoying the rest of your day.

Initially you might require two administration days for every focus day, just to get caught up with your backlogged admin tasks. But eventually, you get to the point where you only need an admin day once a week, or once every other week; the rest of your days can be focus days and spirit days. It is a wonderfully freeing framework.

Once you have gotten completely caught up on your admin, if an admin task comes up on your focus day, you know it will get taken care of on your admin day; it does not have to be addressed in that moment. On your focus day, a lot of the admin stuff will already be done, which means you are not going to be thinking about outstanding admin tasks in the back of your mind. Also, if new admin tasks come up, you know they will get done on your next admin day. This will help you to focus, and because you are focusing, you will get more done, so by the time admin day comes around again, you'll be caught up and will feel free to just do the admin day.

In terms of organizing your physical space, organize according to the way you are going to use things. Many people organize by category, putting all their books here, and all of their pencils there. But you should leave out the things that you use on a regular basis so they are within arm's reach. The things that you use a little less frequently can be placed so that you have to lean over or reach to get them. And the things that you never use can go a few feet away. Always think about how often and why you use an object when you are deciding where to put something. Group things by use rather than by category.

If you are a freelancer, you do not want someone who might hire you to think that you are interrupting your work to take a prospect call, because when the time comes for their job to be done, you do not want them to worry that you are going to be stopping every ten minutes. Keep a good separation between interruptions and scheduled focus work time. That way, if someone does happen to call as an interruption, you can simply schedule an appointment for later.

From interview with Steven Robbins *[www.steverrobbins.com], Stever Robbins, CEO of Ideas Unleashed, and host of the podcast The Get-it-Done Guy's Quick and Dirty Tips to Work Less and Do More.*

One of the biggest challenges we have is to learn how to efficiently manage our time. If we cannot manage our time well, we end up working long hours, often inefficiently, and can easily start despising the work we have, or the freelance career that we so much wanted. Many highly successful translators don't work long or irregular hours. Instead they have learned to manage time efficiently in order to have time for other things in life. Most of you became a freelance translator to enjoy the benefits of being your own boss. To do this, you must proactively manage your time and your clients.

TRACK YOUR TIME

In order to develop and learn time management, we have to know where our time is going, so the first step is to track your time. This may seem counter-productive since it is going to take even more time out of your day, but if we don't know where our time is going, we cannot decide what to do about it or create a plan. There are many different tracking tools. Rescue Time is one the easiest to use. You just install it on the computers you use and it tracks your time on QuickBooks, Trados Studio, Memo Q, Outlook, or working on emails. Then you can categorize these into productive time or non-productive time. Rescue Time does this automatically, but you can tweak the settings to reflect your definition of productivity.

Toggl is another popular tool for proofreading or tracking hourly work. It's an online timer that you can start and stop for the projects you're working on. This way you can keep good track of where your time is going. Other things to consider are how often you are interrupted, and how long it takes to complete certain tasks. Once you have this tracking information, you'll also be able to calculate how much you're making per hour. This can encourage you to become more efficient with your time, instead of just working more hours. After you've seen your personal patterns, and where your time is going,

115

work out what you can outsource, what you should focus on, and what you should probably let go.

TO-DO LISTS

Another tip is to make a list at the beginning of each day of everything that you need to do. Prioritize the tasks – because usually we don't manage to do all the tasks on our to-do list. Number each task in the order you will complete it and make a time estimate for how long you will spend on each one. This will help you keep working at a reasonable pace and ensure that your schedule isn't derailed by any one task. While it's easier said than done, it's good to have a goal. When you've completed a task, cross it off the list – it will feel so good.

GET ORGANIZED

If you can keep an organized office, you won't waste time or be distracted looking for things, so prioritize organization. If you have organized your finances, you won't have to spend time figuring out which clients owe you money and when. If you have an organized schedule, you won't have to waste time between activities. You'll know what you should continue with after finishing a task. Spend the last 15 minutes of every working day organizing your desk, updating client files, doing the invoicing and making your to-do list for the next day. Once you're earning a fairly steady income, you can start focusing on tasks that you do well and try to outsource tasks that you don't like to do, or that take too much of your time and make you unproductive.

Tasks that are useful to outsource are housecleaning, accounting, web design, and small desk publishing tasks. They may be fun to do (for some), but they take up a lot of time. And your time is more efficiently spent translating.

You know how important it is to engage in continual marketing, but this is often a task that gets put to the side. Income-generating tasks get higher priority, but it is important not to forget about marketing, and all other little projects that we want to do, even if they don't have deadlines. Put them in the calendar, otherwise they might never get done, or they might take much longer than they need to.

PRIORITIZE TASKS TO GET THEM DONE

If you tend to not regularly perform your marketing activities, try doing a half hour or so of marketing tasks first thing in the morning. That way they are done, and you can focus on your translating work. Also try to think of ways to take advantage of your smaller pockets of time. Meetings often run late and you must wait, or you wait to pick up your children from practice or the doctor's office. These small pockets of time are perfect for replying to emails and phone calls, preparing for a meeting or confirming appointments. If you focus, you can often get more done in 15 minutes than in one hour of unfocused work.

FOCUS

Focus on one task at a time. Even if we believe that we are efficient multi-taskers, the truth is that multi-tasking is not at all efficient. So focus on one task at a time. One tip is to keep a notebook next to you, so when you think of things unrelated to what you're working on right now, you can make a short note of them, or put them on the to-do list and get back to them later. Perhaps save them for one of those 15-minute pockets mentioned earlier. Another trick to help you focus is to set a timer for 25 to 50 minutes and only focus on one task during that time. When the timer rings you can take a break and check emails, put in a load of laundry, or do something else for 10 to 15 minutes, and then set the timer again.

END YOUR WORKDAY

It's important to have a set ending time for the workday. If you know you have to finish tasks by a set time, you will be more efficient and you will also have something to look forward to. Another tip is to have goals and plan your time around them. It's much easier to stay focused if you are working towards a goal. You can set smaller goals for your week or your day, accomplishing a certain task by a certain time, or plan for long-term goals and break them down to work on them a little bit at a time. It is important to maintain work-life balance and to not get overworked. We are entrepreneurs, or have our own company, so there are always things to do, but it's important for both our health and well-being, and that of our families, to try to keep a balance.

STRESS-RELEASE

Adopt an activity for stress release. Freelance work can be stressful; we have many deadlines and we must deal with difficult clients and last-minute problems. Find an activity that you enjoy, that makes you relax and focus on other things. It could be going for a walk with the dog, going on a run or going to yoga. It's important to take your weekends off; you will have a more successful career. According to studies, activity per hour declines sharply when we work more than 50 hours a week (and it drops more if we work even more). The most successful entrepreneurs and freelancers take their weekends off, and make the most out of that time off, leading to increased efficiency and productivity during the week.

On the weekend, try to disconnect. If you don't remove yourself electronically from work, then you've never really left work. If you make yourself available 24 hours a day, you're exposed to a constant barrage of stress factors that prevent you from refocusing and recharging – which is what you need to do to be more effective when you do work. For example, if you want to disconnect from emails and such, you might have an auto response on your email saying you'll be back in the office next Monday morning. Also, don't leave all your chores for the weekend. Spend half a weekend day doing the grocery shopping and planning for the next week. The weekend should be a time to reflect. Reflection is a powerful tool for improvement. You can think about your job in a relaxed way and possibly see things in a whole new light.

If you have a hard time finding time to exercise during the week, just go for a walk or something like that. Take time to exercise over the weekend to release the soothing neurotransmitters that reduce stress. Go on a long bike ride or a run, and you may find you get a lot of great ideas regarding your work during this time. Also, find a hobby or a passion that you can focus on during the weekend. This might be playing music, reading, writing, painting, or even just playing with your kids.

Your family is more important than your work or career will ever be, and the same goes for friends. If you get sick, or when you get to 80 years old and think back, family and friends usually have the greatest impact on your life. Don't neglect family and friends in favor of work.

Schedule time for travel and to have micro adventures that spice up your life, or at least have something interesting planned for each weekend. Try to wake up at the same time each day, and if you wake up early, take the morning for "me" time rather than plunging into work. If you have little kids, you might need to find some other time to meditate, think, or engage in activities that you're passionate about that will increase your happiness.

Last but not least, use the last hour of the weekend to prepare for the upcoming week. As little as 30 minutes' preparation can yield gains in productivity and reduce stress. Make a list of what you need to accomplish, what meetings you have, what chores you need to do – the week will feel a lot more manageable when you go into it with a plan.

TAKE THE VACATION

Another important activity is to take vacations. Just like everyone else, freelancers need vacations too, but in order to take one we need to plan ahead. We don't get paid vacation days, so we may need to work extra hours just before a vacation, not only to complete all the work, but also to complete a little extra work to maintain our monthly income goal.

Be sure to communicate your vacation schedule and your availability to your clients – it's one of the most important parts of vacation preparation. Even if you are your own boss and don't have to ask for permission to take time off, you can lose clients pretty quickly if you don't forewarn them about when you're going to be gone. Start early to prepare them, weeks in advance. Give your important regular clients three key details: the dates you'll be gone, your availability during that time (for example, if you are completely unavailable, off the grid with no Internet connection, or if you plan to check emails only once a day), and which assignments and tasks will be completed before you go. This is particularly important because it helps manage the expectations of clients and gives them assurance that you will complete the tasks that they have given you. Try to turn in projects early before you leave for vacation, in case revisions are necessary, or for questions and answers about the material. If possible, you want everything to be completed before you go.

The night before you go on a trip, set an out-of-office email response stating that you are on vacation, and that you will be away from email until such and such a time. At least one of your clients will forget that you are on vacation and the out-of-office email acts as a reminder. Also, if anyone contacts you about new work while you're away, the out-of-office message will reassure them that you are not ignoring them. Plan ahead to prevent surprises. The worry of surprises, or emergency situations, or something going wrong is usually what has so many of us checking emails while we are on vacation. It's not necessarily the fear of missing work; it's the fear that someone is going to be disappointed, or frustrated that you aren't immediately able to help them. Good planning helps mitigate that frustration and if you've

120

communicated in advance, your clients will be reassured that all their needs will be taken care of either before you go or when you get back.

The last thing to plan for is returning from vacation. Figure out what your work schedule is going to look like for the week you get back. If you will be starting any new freelance assignments, or have deadlines to meet, put them in the calendar. If you make these plans before you leave, you can jump right back into your work flow without wasting any time, or losing track of something that might had slipped your mind while you were on vacation. Another good tip is to reserve one day, or a chunk of extra time, when you get back to catch up on all the emails that need answering.

From solo episode with Tess Whitty
[www.marketingtipsfortranslators.com/ episode-60-work-life-balance-working-efficiently-and-preparing-for-time-off]

HOW TO GET RID OF DIGITAL CLUTTER

What is digital clutter and how is it slowing us down? You can think of digital clutter as the logical extension of the physical clutter you find on your desk, in your office, and in your home. Even though you can't see all the digital stuff piling up on your devices, it's there and it's taking up just as much time and energy as the physical clutter. Take email, for example. In the average company, employees spend about 15% of their time just processing email. File management in your computers and other devices has been increasingly complicated by the arrival of apps and the notifications that go with them. It has become such a big part of working from a home office that if you don't get your digital clutter under control, it can consume a lot of your time.

DECLUTTERING EMAIL

Email shouldn't stay in your inbox where you look at it again and again trying to decide what you should do with it. The OHIO approach (Only Handle It Once) is very useful. You can apply this principle to so many things, because so many pieces of digital information only require one decision. It doesn't help to delay it.

FILE MANAGEMENT

Create a substructure within a directory for every client with whom you work. The more detailed that substructure is, the easier it will be to find something. You might make a new folder for every year, and then for every month, that you work with a client. You might save instructions, important emails, terminologies, and contracts so they are all together in one place.

ORGANIZING PASSWORDS

Passwords are abundant now and you need to change them frequently for security reasons. It's complicated to keep track of them. Also, you want to keep them in a secure location in case your computer is hacked.

One recommended tool is LastPass, a password management system that stores encrypted passwords in private accounts. Simply having a list of passwords that you keep somewhere because it's easily accessible makes your computer vulnerable to hacking. However, the use of tools such as LastPass depends on how comfortable you are with the technology. It's not helpful if you're not using it. Whatever solution you use, make sure it adheres to the OHIO principle of only handle it once.

PROCRASTINATION AND TACKLING BIGGER PROJECTS

Many of us have bigger projects that we would like to work on – building a website, or creating a marketing plan, or writing a book, or something else for which we rarely find time.

We can make these tasks too big in our minds, and this can lead us to put them off. But once you start breaking it down into much smaller chunks, it doesn't feel so threatening and you can start addressing it.

Once you have an established practice, say as a translator, it's very easy to simply accept one project after another. Often you end up in this routine, yearning for some extra time to develop your business instead of taking on yet another project.

There's a lot of potential to develop your business further by investing some time in working on a website or a blog. You may increase your earning potential and your marketing reach. And that's so much more important than yet another project that will be completed in an hour or two.

No matter how busy you are, you probably have 10 to 15 minutes that you can commit every day. It is okay to start a big web project as an "under construction" site and then, over time, it will get nicer and you will add pictures – everything doesn't have to happen on the first day. It's important to not let that idea of perfection get in your way – it can become a reason for procrastination.

THE FEAST OR FAMINE CYCLE

Evening out the initial fluctuations we experience when we start out as businesspeople should be a long-term goal. Aim to have a pipeline of projects that are lining up as you are working. You must remember to reach out to clients for new projects, even when you are very busy. All freelancing means feast or famine, and we are better off telling ourselves that every day we must do one thing to market our business. In the long run, this will help even out the peaks and valleys. It may seem counterintuitive to spend time on tasks that aren't generating money, but in the long run these actions will generate more money than staying stuck in working on what's right in front of you.

It takes a few years of business experience to learn that the peak days when you're very busy are the perfect days to reach out to new contacts – because you don't have much time and you are probably feeling confident, so you're going to do it effectively. You're in the best possible bargaining position.

From interview with Dorothee Racette *[www.takebackmyday.com], ATA-certified translator and productivity coach and trainer.*

CHAPTER 5 – TOOLS

Productivity and profitably can be improved by finding and correctly using the right tools. This isn't about getting on board with the newest trend or gadget – it's about carefully choosing which tools can work best with the way you work and the way your clients like to interact with you. Once again we've asked established international translators which tools they find invaluable. Their helpful advice has been gleaned from my podcast Marketing Tips for Translators – find out more about these translation professionals at the end of each section.

Just type "going paperless" into Google, and you'll see a lot of information about going green or having an uncluttered desk. While this might be important for some people, I've found the biggest benefit of going paperless is having access to whatever information I need wherever I am.

Going paperless generally involves online storage services, but you can still have certain folders organized and synchronized to your computer. What is important is having a consistent and descriptive naming convention. Put some thought into how you're going to name your documents so that when you're looking for them later you know what to look for. Also, have a folder structure. The important thing with folders is not necessarily to shoehorn your documents into some structure that you found online, but rather to look at your documents and how you work with them and group them into broad categories that way. It may be worth your while to include the client name in the name of the file, so instead of just calling a folder Box or Dropbox, for example, call it Dropbox PO 12345. That way you can quickly find documents for your client without having to dig through the folders. One nice thing about going paperless and having digital documents is that you can search not only by the name of the file, but by the contents of the text inside the files as well. When you put those two tools together, you can instantly narrow in on the document that you are looking for without having to hunt through files and folders.

KEEPING DIGITAL DOCUMENTS SAFE

There are two important things to do if you want to keep digital documents safe. The first is to back them up – make sure you have your documents stored in as many places as possible, at the very least in two locations. One might be on an extra hard drive or storage device plugged into your computer, and the other should be off-site. So if something were to happen at your physical location – fire, flood, or theft – a copy of your work still exists somewhere else.

As far as keeping your documents safe and secure in the cloud, that's a tough one. If you have something that you never want anyone else to see, you must understand that if you're uploading something to a remote server, it's out of your control. So if you really have something that you would never want anyone to see, you're probably better off not uploading it in the first place. There is no way to keep things 100% secure online – it's just not possible.

If you're going to be storing your documents in the cloud, you want to make sure that the service provider you're using encrypts your data. That is going to help you 99.9% of the time, but understand that if you're putting your documents on the cloud, they are out of your control.

As far as security is concerned, the worst thing you can do is to send a document by email. In most cases, an email attachment is not encrypted. You can definitely password protect it, or you could use something like Dropbox or Box. If a document is sensitive, use the secure length sharing functionality versus sending it as an email attachment.

TOOLS

Evernote is easy to use, and it's visual so a lot of people who are not comfortable working with files and folders really like it. This program subtracts a lot of the technical stuff that you don't need to deal with. And it's easy to add information to it, so you can clip web pages, capture information, and drag files into it quickly. Because it's synchronized to Evernote servers that are available everywhere, you can access it from wherever you are. It has very powerful search capabilities as well. The little shortcuts bar in the Mac, Windows or mobile applications comes in handy if you have notes that you need to access a lot, and you can even do helpful things like save your searches.

From interview with Brooks Duncan [*www.documentsnap.com*], *a Chartered Professional Accountant and computer programmer whose company DocumentSnap helps businesses and individuals go paperless.*

PRODUCTIVITY AND ORGANIZATION APPS FOR TRANSLATORS

These days, you can do almost anything from your digital devices. Mobile phones are most popular, but you can do many things from tablets as well. People who travel frequently need to integrate the work they do at home with the work they do while on the road to optimize their time. Sometimes all you need to do that is an app.

Some desktop solutions have a corresponding app for the phone (such as Google Drive, Dropbox, Evernote, etc.); you need to have the desktop-based application when you upload, but then you can upload from a mobile phone as well. Once you have an account it will connect across all your platforms and devices, and sync the content so you can access it from anywhere and anything, even from a laptop that isn't yours. Dropbox is good for big files or for materials that you consult on a regular basis, but you still have to use a computer or a word processor to open files, edit them and then upload them again to save them.

With Google Drive you need to be online, but you can update something from the app using a mobile phone, and then convert whatever you have created into a PDF or Word file. It has a dimension of evolution that Dropbox doesn't have, so you can use it to create documents from scratch. On Dropbox you can only import documents that you've created previously. So you can have most of the materials that don't need to change, or most of the references from your ongoing jobs on Dropbox, and anything that needs editing can be started on Google Drive, and then converted to a permanent file on Dropbox.

Many translators still like to carry a thumb drive even though they have all their folders synced online. Having files on this portable storage option is especially useful for conferences or meetings. You can also copy yourself on all communications – if you have an IMAP account, you don't get any duplicates, but you still have access to all the messages.

Invoicing requires flexibility, so consider tools for payments such as PayPal or something similar that you can connect to your invoicing system. Your clients get a link to click on, and they can pay from PayPal if they want to be redirected to that platform.

For general organization, Google Drive is great for shared content and ongoing projects. If a few people are working with you on the same project, you can create a group. Of course, this can be done on Facebook, Trello or Basecamp as well.

Google Drive is good for hosting the folders you create and share with people, and it can be either private or public. It meshes with Google Calendar, also part of the Google platform. You can schedule everything from appointments to meetings, jobs to deliver, or goals to meet, and you can set alerts and notifications. For instance, if you set an alarm for 8 pm, it will create an event on both your mobile phone calendar and on your desktop. Sometimes the simplest apps can help you be really efficient.

Now that almost everything is online, you can create your own documents and consult them through Google Drive or Dropbox. If you don't normally work on projects that require repeat terminology, you still need to follow specific requirements and technologies that create terminology to ensure that the brand is consistent. For this, interpreters have created terminology apps. They can help you build your terminology database with a double entry system. You could have Swedish on one side and English on the other, and you could categorize your materials and create a folder each for environment, such as energy, oil and gas, or whatever you're translating, and then just click on the app and see it.

From interview with Valeria Aliperta

[www.rainylondontranslations.com], a UK-based professional conference interpreter and translator, and founder of Rainy London Translations.

GETTING TO INBOX ZERO

If getting to Inbox Zero is your primary goal, there are lots of ways of achieving that. However, for most of us, it's not the absolute number that matters. What matters is that having a well-managed inbox implies that we are using our time well. Email should never overwhelm us. But if you are simply doing a one-off purge, what is described here will get you closer to zero too; get you closer to a fresh start. Once you do get it to zero, see how long you can keep it clear for!

Some routinely aim for inbox zero because it gets email correspondence off the task list. Responding to emails quickly prevents having to add them to a task list. Another type of person who might aim to get to zero more than most is those who find it hard to concentrate well on important things like big translation projects when an inbox is full of little things that have to be done. Getting rid of them is better that being distracted by their mere existence.

Some people swear by checking for messages only once an hour or so. Others check frequently for new email at the times of day when customers tend to write to us; frequent email messages are the nature of our business, after all. You might want to disable audible notifications that indicate new emails though; a small, discreet visual icon that's not going to pop up in the middle of the screen might be less distracting. So email need not interrupt you, but you that can check for the indicator in your task bar if you take a moment to look.

SEPARATE INBOXES

Start by splitting things up; have multiple boxes for personal and professional email. That way if you are working hard and getting those messages off your plate, an email from a friend that needs a chatty reply will not distract you while you are working. For long stretches of your working day, you might not look at your personal email inbox. Every so often, tackle it. It might not get to zero as often as your professional inbox, but perhaps that is fine.

ACTIONABLE OR NOT?

If it's in your inbox, here's the rule: decide whether the email is actionable or not. If it will take you less than two minutes to respond, do it as soon as you read it. Then remove it from your inbox and put it in the appropriate folder, or delete it. Sometimes you can reply and delete, or forward and delete.

That will handle much email. Now, if it is not actionable, or not something that involves you directly – let's say it's a monthly newsletter from a translation association – nothing happens if you ignore or delete these emails, but you might want to spend a few minutes reading them in case they include useful references or dates you should note. That might take more than two minutes; it might take you 5 or 10 minutes to read that item properly. So either leave it there for a while and try and read it that day during a tea break, or turn it into a task, say to read it sometime this week. It depends on your personal preference whether you leave it in your inbox to make sure you do read it, or whether you move it into a "To be read" folder or similar. (Watch out – those can become huge never-ending pits of unread messages.)

Messages that remain in your inbox become tasks or calendar items. Sometimes you are being asked to join a volunteer effort and you need to reflect before you respond. You might put that on the task list or you might add a task to talk or email someone else about it – something that needs to be done before you can respond to the first message.

131

Sometimes you have a firm purchase order for an editing job where you expect the files first thing tomorrow. Put that message as a calendar item and block out the right amount of time for tomorrow, and move the email to the customer's folder. If it is a job that you accept and could do any time over the next few days, create a task right away with the appropriate priority or deadline, and move the message to the customer's folder. In MS Outlook, you simply drag the message to the Calendar or Task tab as appropriate to achieve this. Gmail has a task function too. Others find Evernote or MS OneNote or similar tools useful.

FILTERS

Don't use filters for things that are completely unimportant. You can just delete those unimportant emails after skimming them briefly. Many have mailing list emails go directly into folders. This is email that isn't for you personally but that you might want to respond to or save for later. Some use daily digests for this type of message so that they don't receive these types of emails individually.

To get to inbox zero, you really have to have a pretty quick delete finger. There's no point in keeping 17 back issues of a newsletter that you haven't read. If your inbox is full of that kind of thing, sort it by "From" and delete all but the newest one. You know you're not going to go back and read them all. And if you have 17 unread back issues, then perhaps you should consider unsubscribing.

Using a combination of these techniques should clean up your inbox. We all have to apply them when we return from trips or time off, when we don't keep up with email to nearly the same extent. Those are also good times to unsubscribe to messages that you have found yourself deleting more than reading recently. So set up your folders, keep your finger on the delete button, and go for it! Maybe you'll be at Inbox Zero soon!

Derived from an interview with Karen Tkaczyk

[www.mcmillantranslation.com], a PhD chemist, French into English technical translator, and editor, specializing in chemistry.

HOW TO USE A WEBSITE TO MARKET YOUR TRANSLATION SERVICES

A website is of no use if you don't know why you have it. The first question you should ask is, when someone visits my website, what is their experience? Many successful companies are content with providing informational content to their visitors without engagement, but wouldn't you prefer to turn a website visitor into a customer, or at least a lead? Designing your website around user engagement can turn it into a powerful marketing tool.

PLANNING THE WEBSITE

Before you start creating a website, a little planning will go a long way. Think about the following: What's the purpose of your website? Perhaps it could function as an online marketing brochure, a place where people can read more about your services. Thanks to SEO, you won't have to go out and search too hard for clients – they will find you. How will the people who visit your website benefit from it? Do you want to just provide more information about yourself? Do you have an easy way for them to contact you? Are you selling your services on the site? You should also think about the content, what kinds of information and features you want to include. Consider identifying some appropriate keywords before you start working on your website. It's easy to research these with several of the handy online tools that are available. For example, with Google Ads, there's a Google keyword tool to generate some basic words that describe your services.

133

You should also give some consideration to your domain name. It should be easy to spell, easy to say, and not be too lengthy. For example, the domain name "Swedish Translation Services" is long, but it clearly describes what is being provided as a service. Next, choose a web host. You can host your own site, or pay a provider for hosting, or you can use the hosting services provided by content management systems such as WordPress. Once you've thought about these things, choose a provider or a website building service and start looking at their templates. Most are free and very good-looking. Custom templates are available for a fee if you want more than just services. But consider customizing your templates so that everything looks the way you want it to. Add your own content, pictures, and your logo if you have one. That's it! You are ready to publish.

CONTENT

All websites have a homepage, or a landing page where you should post your best copy to convince people to read further. Include your unique selling points here. It's also good to have an ABOUT page that describes you and your business, or company history. Most people like to buy from people they know and trust. If you include information about yourself, readers will feel like they know you better. You can have a separate page for the services you offer, such as translation, proofreading, or desktop publishing, with or without pricing information. Having a separate contact page with all your contact details is also useful. There should be a call to action or a contact button on every page, but also include a separate contact page that's easy to find. Another page could include samples of your translations, references, or testimonials. You can also provide links to useful translation resources or client resources, and a page for events. If you provide training or if you've attended training, it's good to list these credentials to show people that you care about continuing education. You can also list your certifications. If you publish articles, make your samples multilingual to show that you are a multilingual website and business. This is actually one of the hardest things in the whole creation process. However, it is important, and the easiest way to do it is just to link two sites together, or to have a subdomain with your other language content.

DESIGN

Website design has some basic rules. It's good to have a call to action (a link or button that tells the visitor what to do after they have read about you or your services on the website) on each page. These should appear "above the fold," on the most prominent areas of the site, rather than be hidden in the footer. This call to action can say "contact me for a free quote" or "contact me to get more information about my services today." Focus on legibility by using clear fonts and lots of white space. Use headings and an index or menu with a structure that is clear and easy to navigate. Use bullet points within the text, because people don't have long attention spans – if you use large headings and bullet points, it's easier to see what the content is about. Of course, try to make the colors match or complement one another. If you use a template, this usually occurs automatically.

For the text, remember to use short paragraphs. People don't have time to read long, rambling texts. For each page you should use unique and concise, but meaningful, titles or title tags. Title tag generation will be included in most popular design templates. Titles should be 60 to 80 characters long because this is the limit for search engines. The best title tag would be something that coincides with the search phrase you want potential customers to use to find your website. It should convey what your webpage is about. Place the most important pages in a root or main folder, and less important pages into sub folders. Try to make your site user-friendly for your clients and potential clients. Write for your potential clients and show them how you can provide value to them.

Another tip is to place a search bar on each page of your site. Visitors can easily find the information they need instead of having to click around to find it. If you want to make the website even more attractive in SEO terms, you can add a forum or a blog. Lots of translators have blogs these days, but you don't have to. You can just provide a page for updating customers, telling them when you are going to be on vacation, or mentioning a new course you're taking. This is an easy way to update the website often, which the search engines appreciate.

There are a few things to avoid. Don't use crazy formats and colors. Don't use predictable or boring content. Don't steal content – always write your own copy. Don't let your site get stale –update it often. Broken links and missing images look sloppy – make sure everything works on all browsers. Do not just write about yourself; write about how you can help clients. We are translators and proofreaders, so we definitely should have websites free of grammar mistakes. Proofread, proofread, proofread – and ask other people to proofread your website too. Pop-ups, irritating animations, and flash elements are things to avoid.

SEARCH ENGINE MARKETING

Search engine marketing uses a mix of online marketing strategies to help users easily find you online. Did you know that 80% of online users employ search engines to find a product or service? Out of these, 58% tend to trust a company with web presence more than a company without a website. Google different translator websites to see what's out there and you'll see that the optimized websites offer a big competitive advantage. People will typically search by someone's name, company name, product name, or with keywords, which could be the type of expertise they're looking for in translation services, types of products or services, or the language they're seeking. Your goal is to be referenced on the first page of search results when someone searches for any information that is relevant to you or your business.

However, getting to the top of search results requires work and an overall understanding of what it takes to compete online. Here are three things to remember when you optimize your website:

- You should always be thinking about your buyers, your sales process, and the search engines. Design your website in a way that grabs your visitors' attention and keeps them while they make their first split-second decision to get in touch, or inquire about services. Include the information they need to clearly understand how you can help them with what you specifically offer. Make sure that your site is appealing and easy to navigate. Navigation is a key feature, so provide easy-to-find tabs, link between the pages, and provide a search field.

- Make sure your site is search-engine-friendly and includes the keywords that you're using to find your target market. Title tags or metatags are important, so update them and use them. Be aware that robots use keyword and description tags to index and rank your site on the Internet. Ensure that each of your content's internal links – links between pages, image tags and titles, and headings on the page – are using the relevant keywords that can help with your ranking.

- Embed an analytic tracking tool such as Google Analytics in your site. Check your statistics regularly, or have Google send a report to you weekly. The great thing about search engine marketing is that it's very measurable. You can track the number of visitors that come to your site, where they came from, and how long they stayed, or even which pages they visited or stayed on the longest. You can compare the number of visitors to the number of leads you get in a month to measure conversion rates from visitor to lead.

MARKETING AND PROMOTING YOUR WEBSITE

Once you have optimized your site, you are ready to start driving traffic to it. This involves off-site promotion and driving leads, contacts and visitors back to specific web pages where they can take action.

Many simple and inexpensive ways are available to market your website online. You can put a link to your website in your email signature. You can include a link to your website when you post to news groups, forums or discussion groups. You should always include a link to your website in all your online profiles and directories. For example, if you are a member of the ATA, or have a ProZ.com profile, make sure you include a link to your website there. Also, if you have social media accounts – Facebook, Twitter, LinkedIn – include a link to your website.

Don't forget to market your website offline as well. You can have a link to your website on your business cards, on your resume, on your brochure if you have one, on your Christmas cards – you get the idea.

There are also special tools to integrate your website with your different social media platforms. Many website service providers offer these as options or opt-ins. For example, in WordPress you can add buttons so people can follow you on social media, or share the content on your website with others. If you write blog posts, you can also add share buttons so people can distribute your content to colleagues and friends.

- Start by submitting your site to the various search engines and directories. The most popular ones are Google, Yahoo and Bing. Don't forget to get on local search directories to build a local presence, because they are very effective at getting you to the top of the search rankings quickly. If somebody is looking for an interpreter or translator in Chicago, for example, and you are listed in the local search directory, you will be right up there.

- Make short videos or presentations and put them on YouTube and other popular video sharing sites. Take note that YouTube is the second biggest search engine after Google, so having a video on that platform can be very beneficial.

- Another tip is to write articles and post them in article directories. Also, search for blogs in your subject area and in the translation industry, then participate by commenting or guest posting to build credibility and exposure, and to drive readers to additional information on your site. You can link to your site from your comments and posts.

- When someone finds your website, it's important to engage them. When a potential customer arrives at your website, whether it is via a search engine or a link from a translation association directory or some other list, they will look first for information about you. One of their first questions will be whether your language combination and subject field matches their requirements. The next thing the potential customer is going to want to determine from the website is whether you are credible. At this point in the sales cycle a potential customer knows what you do, but still doesn't know whether he or she can trust you. Are you really the great translator you say you are? Do you really deliver the accurate and reliable translations you say you do? The potential customer is going to start looking around on the website for evidence that these statements are true. Most people say they provide high-quality, on-time translations – you need to stand out, and provide proof and reassurance to potential customers.

PROVIDING PROOF OF YOUR SKILLS

Many ways exist to prove our value to potential customers. You can include testimonials on your website, since the word of others (particularly happy customers) is much more effective than your own subjective statements. You can write a blog, not for translators, but one that is specific to another subject or field, but with a focus on translation and your customers. Use this as an opportunity to demonstrate your knowledge, and to position yourself as an expert in your field. If you are certified, make sure that this is easy to see for a customer visiting your website. Another approach is to provide interesting and useful information that potential customers can download and use. This is where you can interest them enough to give you their name in exchange for information of value to them.

Let's say you have an information product that the potential customer is interested in and wants. They can get it by signing up with an email address. You can then use an automated process to follow up and keep in touch with them. You can send messages and provide them with tips, advice and news about your latest projects, and entice them in your follow-up emails to take action and engage with you. A great tool for this is Aweber, an email marketing tool that creates lists of subscribers.

All of these methods provide opportunities for you to show that you know what you're talking about, and this is what will ultimately convince a potential customer that you are the right person for the job.

Search engine marketing is not a magic bullet or a get-rich-quick scheme. It's a marketing tool that every business professional needs to use as part of their growth and competitive strategy. The more you understand the bigger picture, what drives the effectiveness of search engine marketing, the easier it is to execute the detail. Keeping the customer in mind is of utmost importance.

Based on solo episode with Tess Whitty
[www.marketingtipsfortranslators.com/episode-40-use-website-market-translation-services]

USING INFORMATION PRODUCTS TO ADD VALUE TO YOUR WEBSITE

A website provides potential clients with information about who you are and what you do, and about the services you offer, without them actually having to contact you.

Most potential clients can find and access translators' association directories, but without a website you are just a name, a telephone number and an address on a list. When we look for products and services in our personal or professional lives, we usually go online for information before we call a particular service provider. We want to know whether they are a good fit, or if they provide a product that we really want. That is why it is very important for translators to have a website. Of course, there are alternatives to websites such as a LinkedIn profile, or other kinds of profiles; however, those are preferably extras, rather a substitute for a website.

HOW TO PROVIDE MORE VALUE TO A WEBSITE

We must ask the question, what are our clients looking for when they go to our website? The answer is, first of all, information. They may have a translation requirement and they want to see if what you offer is what they need. If the answer is yes, they're going to move on to a second point, which is, do you look like a reliable professional person who can provide a decent translation and good service? They are likely looking for evidence that you are trustworthy, that you know what you are doing, and that you have expertise in the area in which they need translation.

If we want to provide value, we should address these two questions and provide the information for which clients are looking, and then give proof of reliability. There are several ways to do this, and here are a few things to think about:

- Testimonials from satisfied customers are very useful. You can say you are a reliable translator and never miss a deadline, but someone else's word is better than yours.

- Writing a blog gives you a chance to show off your expertise and it shows potential clients that you know what you're talking about, because not only can you do the translation, you can discuss the issues.

A TYPICAL SALES CYCLE FOR POTENTIAL CLIENTS THAT FIND YOUR WEBSITE

A potential client will come across your name somewhere and find your website address in the search engine, or on a directory list. They will come to your website if they are looking for translation. Some people are pretty quick at making decisions, or perhaps they already have a recommendation from somebody, so they just send you a proposal. Other potential clients don't know you at all and are going to need much more proof that you are trustworthy, reliable, and credible before they even think about sending you an inquiry.

The more sensitive and important the translation is for this potential client, the more information and proof they are going to want from you before they give you their text. So, where are they going to go looking for that proof when they don't yet know you and you are just a name on a list? They're going to go to your website. And if they don't find any proof there, then they're going to go somewhere else.

BUILDING TRUST

Providing information products on your website is a good strategy. Maybe it's a guide, or a flyer, or maybe a list of courses, or articles and other products that are interesting or useful (or even valuable) to both existing and potential clients.

While it will be time-consuming to write them, once you do, you'll have these materials forever. You can always add and update, so it is a long-term activity. You can make materials downloadable to start, and have them in printed versions for direct marketing and for various other purposes.

*From interview with **Karen Rueckert** [www.legal-translations-rueckert.com], a legal translator based in Germany.*

143

SEO TIPS FOR TRANSLATORS

Search engine optimization (SEO) is the art of organically boosting the ranking of your website or page or blog on Google, Yahoo or Bing. Ranking better organically means that it happens naturally, not by cheating with keyword stuffing, or by buying advertising. Advertising on Google is obviously a search engine optimization method, but we have all seen ads on Google – ask yourself how often you click on them. At the end of the day, search engine optimization is about being found. However, being on page one of search results does not mean clients will pour in, so keep expectations realistic.

However, if you are a freelance translator and you went to the trouble and invested money in having a professionally-made website, and it is not optimized for search engines – that is just sad. A direct client or an agency will not look on ProZ.com, or in a translator directory. They do not even know that translators' directories exist. The average marketing manager for a big company does not care about that. They need a translator, and basically they are going to turn to Google – in the same way we all "google" products that we need. That is why it is important to rank high on searches.

KEYWORDS

Keywords are not as important as they used to be, but they are not dead. Keywords are still important. Google wants to deliver the right content to the right user in the right moment, so they've drastically changed the way their algorithms work.

The new algorithms are no longer keyword-based; they are question-based. If you ask a question on Google, you'll notice the results are starting to be more and more accurate. This is the efficiency of semantic or contextual search.

For example, if I am searching for an English to Swedish medical translator, the words "English to Swedish medical translator" would be a long tail keyword, and the word "translator" would be a short tail keyword. It is much better to rank on page one and to focus your efforts on ranking extremely well for "English to Swedish medical translator" than it is just for "translator" or "Swedish translator." A long tail keyword is several words grouped together instead of just one or two words. It's more specific, and it tends to give better results. I recommend that anybody with a website use Google Webmaster Tools. These are extremely powerful and user-friendly tools that tell you about the health of your website, and offer tips on how to improve your SEO as well.

What this means for translators is that you can focus much less on keywords themselves, and concentrate instead on including meta tags and meta keywords for your pages. Making people-friendly content is making Google-friendly content. But do not create that content with Google in mind; create content with your readers in mind. That way the content will be relevant and your readers can share it all across social networks and platforms.

NEW RULES ABOUT OPTIMIZATION FOR GOOGLE

1. Google loves social networking shares and links, and likes on Facebook, because they want to deliver the right content at the right moment to the right person. The algorithm is a machine, not a human being. At least for now, the only way that this machine can judge whether content is good or bad is by counting human shares and likes. Basically, it decides that if an article on your blog has a lot of shares or likes, it must be good, so it is worth ranking higher.

2. Good content is the foundation of SEO because users share and link to it, which they do not do for bad content. Being known for having good content is good for your reputation within the industry, and you'll establish yourself more readily as the expert in whatever area you are writing on.

From interview with Anne Diamantidis

[www.marketingtipsfortranslators.com/episode-32-latest-seo-tips-translator-websites-interview-anne-diamantidis]

BLOGGING FOR TRANSLATORS

Many translators have started blogging. Some feel that it's a necessary part of their content marketing for their translation business, others blog mostly for networking with colleagues and sharing their insights on languages, translation and interpreting. Most translation bloggers love the way having a blog connects them with colleagues from all over the world, and with clients too.

BLOGGING FOR CLIENTS

Try to blog regularly about the events you are attending. Especially for localization translation events, a blog is a good medium for connecting with potential clients who will also be at those events. Guest posts written for other blogs are also useful for marketing purposes, especially those published in non-translation blogs. Guest blogging about translation and language for potential clients' blogs is a good way to establish contact.

HOW TO START A BLOG

It's a good idea to try guest posting first. It's a great way to see if you enjoy writing, and if readers enjoy your style, which is also important. If you don't like writing, contributing to a blog may not be one of your best marketing tools. Bear in mind that it is time-consuming to start and maintain a blog. It can feel a bit overwhelming during the first few months and most bloggers just stop feeding their blog with new posts after some months.

Even if you don't feel like writing, you can still collect good ideas about potential blog posts whenever they occur to you. Keep a notebook or file. Then when it's time to post, just choose one idea, and sit down and write about it. Not every article has to be 2000 or 3000 words. If you have something useful or interesting to say, it doesn't have to be long, thoroughly researched, or even organized. Translators' off-the-cuff thoughts are actually very interesting for colleagues to read.

Before launching the blog, you should have at least 10 posts ready to go. An editorial calendar will prevent you from feeling overwhelmed in the first two or three months and it will give you the time and freedom to get used to having a blog and get into the rhythm of posting.

Be social and reachable. If people can't reach you through your blog, then what is the purpose of having one? Have lots of buttons for posting comments and for sharing posts on social media.

Lastly, don't forget plugins, because they can be lifesavers. There are many available for blogs, and most of them are free. They can take care of things like SEO, monitoring comments and keeping out spam, showing related posts on your blog, and social sharing. A good plugin can do almost all the work for you.

From interview with Catherine Christaki [www.linguagreca.com], a specialist in Greek technical translations, and co-founder of Lingua Greca Translations.

Imagine LinkedIn as a big, unlimited, virtual trade show or conference where all your clients are hanging out. You basically do what you would do if you were attending this conference or trade show in person – identify people, contact them, start a discussion. There are many ways to market your services on LinkedIn, but a good starting point is your profile. It's your welcome mat to your LinkedIn account. Start by building an optimized profile, and then get proactive. Participate in groups, invite people, show yourself off as an expert, and get networking. LinkedIn has tricky netiquette (the unwritten rules of a social network) with very strict rules. Many people do not realize this, and they do not use LinkedIn the way they should.

PROFILE

The first thing you have to ask is who are your target clients? With that in mind, provide a good picture and a good headline (which should at the very least show your language spheres and specialty skills). A translator can be much more than just a translator. For example, if you specialize in chemistry and you have a PhD, you may want your clients to know about these credentials right away. These are the kinds of things you should put in your headline. Anything that makes you different from your competition is worth mentioning up front.

When creating your profile, just write as if you are writing a resume or cover letter, or as you would explain what you do to someone if you were trapped together in an elevator for ten minutes. Do not think about keywords; imagine that you have a potential client reading your profile and they are completely uneducated about what you do. They have no idea how your industry works, and they do not care. They just need you for a service. How are you going to explain to them what you do, and why you are the person they need?

148

COMMON MISTAKES

A very common mistake in our industry is treating a LinkedIn profile as if it's a CV. Your LinkedIn profile should contain everything you cannot put in your CV. A LinkedIn profile is your entire professional history written by yourself – storytelling is the key word here. Write your history as a professional and as a person.

Too many colleagues write their profiles in the third person. That's a faux pas in LinkedIn etiquette, because the convention is to write your own profile. Writing in the third person goes against the goal of your LinkedIn profile, which is to create a social relationship with people, or to network with them.

GROUPS

It makes no sense for you to be in a translators group. You should be in your end clients' industry groups. These groups are full of potential prospects. Start discussions in the group that are not always centered on what you do as a translator.

USING THE SEARCH FUNCTION

If your primary targets are agencies, you should focus on the hardcore vendor managers, or project managers. Search for project managers, and then use the LinkedIn search function to target the exact industry.

For those seeking end client contacts, most of the time you want to identify the regular sales manager. This is usually the person in charge of translation. However, in some industries it could be the marketing manager, sales manager, communications manager, or the vice president of sales. Use the search function to identify potential clients or prospects. You need to identify the industry on which you want to focus, and then within this industry identify who to go to for translation services.

It may be online networking, but at the end of the day the rules do not change. It is exactly the same thing as in-person networking. Be active, but whatever you would not do offline, do not do online. Behave on LinkedIn as you would networking with prospective clients at industry conferences.

CONNECTING

The least you can do is to take five minutes to write a customized message to a potential client or connection. Try saying that you read or liked someone's blog post as an icebreaker. Getting requests from complete strangers and people who are not in your industry can be off-putting. Why would you respond to them if they do not even bother to take the time to tell you why they want to connect with you?

From interview with Anne Diamantidis
[www.marketingtipsfortranslators.com/episode-32-latest-seo-tips-translator-websites-interview-anne-diamantidis]

Google+ is a huge platform with many products that are more or less connected to each other. There's not much agreement on how it really helps in terms of search engine marketing, but Google+ allows a lot of flexibility when you want to post your own content.

Your business community and your potential customers are spread over many platforms. Any translator who wants to have a comprehensive marketing strategy needs to look into all of the major platforms, and Google+ should be one of these.

SEO

You can use a Google+ search in two different ways. You can use it while you're logged into your account so some of the search results might actually indicate whether your contacts have also liked or circled or visited or rated some of those search results already. However, most people use the search function without being logged in to Google+.

If you use Google+ to link to your other accounts, it might influence the rankings of your sites, and maybe your personal blog, in a positive way. But, whether that works or not is unclear. You should always have a comprehensive online strategy and not rely on any one channel alone. Google+ is relatively young and not as clearly successful as some other products. But Google changes and improves it every few weeks or months, and you never know when a substantial change to the platform will be instituted that could indeed help you with search engine rankings. You don't want to, as they say, come late to the party – make sure you have already established a circle of friends and colleagues in Google+.

CONTENT-CENTRIC

Google+ focuses a lot on content. You can find very interesting articles, pictures and other content through the search function, or with hashtags, rather than through people's profiles. It seems like users on Google+ concentrate more on common interests than on personal relationships.

GOOGLE+ PAGE

If you start a Google+ page, you can link it to your personal website and then link back, telling Google that it's a complementary channel that goes along with your blog. As with other channels you might use for your networking or SEO strategy, if you use similar names or URLs, and keep linking properly, you can bolster all of your channels. And if you post a teaser, or maybe even excerpts from your article on Google+, and you have circles that notice when you have a new article, they might comment on your Google+ article instead of on your blog or website, and thereby spread the word among all of their circles and channels.

GOOGLE+ GROUPS

You can actually join these communities not just as an individual person, but also as a company entity on Google+. Most of these communities allow a convenient way of discussing and communicating on different topics.

Some groups deal only with translation, while others are about translation and localization. It makes sense for translators to look a little bit beyond those communities to groups that deal with linguistics or language tips, research and certain technologies. If you're active in healthcare, for example, try to find a group that deals with that sector. These groups may not obviously be about translation, but you might find help with certain terminology or other aspects of the content that you're translating. Use the top search on Google+, but also the communities search bar on the left side of the window. This is a good way to discover other people, companies and entities that you might never have found otherwise.

GOOGLE+ PROFILE VERSUS PAGE

Both options make sense. It very much depends on how you distinguish your personal life from your professional life as a freelancer. This prompts some organizational questions, but it's also a cultural question. For example, Europeans distinguish a lot more between their private lives and professional lives, whereas professionals in the US don't do that as much.

Using a page rather than a profile makes more sense in terms of branding. But if you want to use Google+ for personal use and for your translation business at the same time (but you don't like mixing the two), then it makes sense to set up a page for your business activity.

A lot of translators established a fairly good network on Google+ even before the pages feature came along. Some of them had to start building a network all over again. Consider what your strategy looks like and how you want to communicate online, how much you're doing this as a person, and how much as a business entity. Being a business is quite different from being a regular person with some translation jobs on the side.

The advantage of having a page is that at some point you may make a career change. So if you as a person pick up a different job, you can always just leave the Google+ page alone, since it is your translation activity.

From interview with Sebastian Hasselbeck *[www.sebastian-haselbeck.de], a technology policy advisor, author and digital entrepreneur living in Berlin.*

153

Google Ads fall into the category of targeted traffic, and it's important to understand what that means. Back in the old days, people would advertise using posters and display ads in newspapers, and they could never really tell which advertising strategy was working. In fact, there's a famous saying that goes, "I know that half of my advertising works, but I don't know which half." There's a frustration in not being able to track what actually works in your business. With the Internet, it's a lot different. You can easily track everything that is happening.

With Google Ads, you are not just advertising randomly; you're directing your advertisements at a particular market. When you type something into Google, you will notice that there are different types of results at the top, and sometimes on the right-hand side, and sometimes at the bottom – this is paid advertising content. In other words, two different types of search results appear: those that are paid results, and organic or natural traffic results.

To get an organic listing, you can perform activities such as search engine optimization. But how can you position yourself in the paid results, and why would you want to? This is not a traditional type of advertising, such as in a newspaper where you might pay $500 for the advertisement, but you don't know how many people will actually look at it. On Google, you don't actually pay unless someone clicks on your ad.

The target for Google Ads is usually going to be your website. But you might not want that ad click to go to your homepage, for example. You might want it to go to a contact form, or a specific signup form, or a landing page where you can actually convert the user into a lead. Someone coming to the homepage might just have a quick look around and leave. Someone landing on a page that offers an immediate quote might be more likely to fill in their details, and then you are actually starting a business relationship with that person.

The idea is to get them to a particular place on the website where they can sign up or submit their request for a quote right away. How you set this up depends on what you're hoping to accomplish. If you're an interpreter rather than a translator, it might be slightly different. It really depends on what you're looking to achieve.

HOW TO GET STARTED

The first thing you need is a Google email address, which is free to set up. Then, you log in to Google AdWords with your Gmail address and simply work your way through the process.

The system is generally easy to use, but it can also be quite complicated. It's fairly easy to set up a basic campaign, but there are all kinds of tweaks and variations you can add.

The first thing that you want to do when you pull up the Google AdWords screen is to click on the red button that says new campaign. Several options will come up: search network with display select, search network only, display network only, and a couple of other variations. Ask yourself if you want your adverts to appear in Google search when someone types in "French translator," for example, or if you want your ads to appear somewhere on other people's sites.

Google AdWords will take you through a range of options if you want your ad to appear on people's websites. Type in a campaign name, then enter the location. You can set your campaign to appear in a particular location, or you can have it appear all around the world, or just in selected countries. You can also have it appear only on pages that use certain languages.

How much are you prepared to pay per click? This is really important because it's where people get concerned about what's going on and how much money they are spending. Many people put in a default bid of something like $0.50 a click, just to get started. You can always change it later. Then, put in an overall budget for a particular campaign.

Let's say you're looking to spend $2 a day, which is $60 a month. Be careful, because it can become quite expensive if you don't manage pricing carefully. However, it can also bring you a lot of business. It's about finding that balance.

As results start to come in, you'll see how much you're actually paying to run your ads and you can adjust the formula. You need to monitor the campaign for the first few days and weeks to see what people have clicked on, what search terms people are putting in, and how much it's costing you per click. Then you can start adjusting.

MONITORING THE CAMPAIGN

Log in first thing in the morning and check what happened the previous day, and then make any necessary adjustments. You might see that you've paid $1.80 for a particular term, and you might think that's too much, so lower the maximum daily spending limit. You might not get as much coverage, but you will control your costs. You can link a credit card to the account in order to pay or prepay. If you're not sure, just set a daily limit of $1. It's not going to be worth doing it if you're not ready to come up with $1 or $2 per day; think of it as an investment. So you can spend $100, as long as you're earning back more than that.

SETUP

Picking good keywords is very important. You can use the Google Keyword tool and the system will suggest keywords for you.

Then you will need to design your advertisement. The first thing the program asks is that you type in the URL of a webpage or landing page, and then it will ask you to write your ad, which is four lines long. There's a headline, so you might put something like "best French translator" followed by the words "quick, cheap" and "great value" or "high quality" or whatever you feel should be highlighted. Then add a couple of lines for text. Check out the sample ads provided – they are very concise. Finally, it goes off for approval by Google, which doesn't take very long, perhaps a few hours.

TWEAKING FOR RESULTS

Google currently has three settings for keywords. Once you've set up your ad, you can go in and review your keywords; in one of the columns you will see the keyword match type. There are three match types: exact, phrase match and broad match. **Exact match** means that your ad will run only if the term someone types into search matches your keyword exactly. For example, if they type in "French translator" as a keyword, then it will show your ad, and if they click on it, you'll pay. It won't acknowledge similar words; they must be exactly the same. The **broad match** is very broad, as the name implies; sometimes you will get clicks, but you may be paying for people who are not really looking for a French translator at all. They might even be looking for things like a French café in New York. People don't always read the ads carefully before clicking on them, and yet you still have to pay for their inattention. However, broad matches can also bring in more business, because people will type in something that you haven't thought of that can bring a client to your site. **Phrase match** is a trade-off between exact match and broad match. Instead of "French translator," the keywords might be "French Translator New York" or "Best French Translator." It tends to pick up results that are closer to what you're looking for.

Generally speaking, it's probably safest to go for exact match. You will get fewer clicks, and you will pay less, and you will know that the people who click on your site are really looking for what you are offering.

So focus on longer tail keywords and don't compete with the masses. You really only need to be competing with people in your particular niche, not millions of people. But the more you can focus on accurate

157

long tail keywords, and on your specific services, the better your chances of success. What do you really offer? Do you offer translation? Do you offer French to English translation, or do you offer French to English financial translation? And so on.

From interview with Paul Urwin [www.100percentlanguages.com], *a languages entrepreneur, speaker, coach, digital author and CEO of 100% Languages.*

CHAPTER 6 – INTO THE FUTURE

After reading this book, perhaps you are well on your way to establishing yourself as a freelance translator and language specialist. But building a business – even with a staff of one – is a long-term proposition. This chapter offers insights into maintaining and improving your translation business into the future. Once again, I offer some of my own favorite strategies, along with tips from experts I've interviewed for my podcast, Marketing Tips for Translators – find out more about these translation professionals at the end of each section.

There are three lessons that hold the magic key to becoming a world-class translator: humility, collaboration and perseverance.

HUMILITY

As we approach a text, we must be humble to its potential. As translators, we are required to climb into the mind of the author; to have the same knowledge of the world and the same subject-matter expertise. The translator must know everything the original author knows. This is an enormously demanding requirement. It's important that we are humble because, on any given day, someone out there may be producing a better translation than ours – in fact, many more people may be doing so. This industry is jam-packed full of talent, especially in the premium market. So humility must underlie everything we do.

COLLABORATION

Collaboration encounters enormous resistance in our industry, where work tends to be isolated. The industry attracts translators who work by themselves, and the lack of collaboration tends to drive down pricing. While agencies may want translations to get done, they often fail to review the completed work, usually as a way to cut costs or win work at lower end-client rates. Increasingly, agencies either do not review the work, or they have an unqualified person do so. It's difficult for translators to learn from un-reviewed work – you are translating all by yourself and it's a one-way process. You may be making the same mistakes repeatedly, and they are not being caught by an unqualified linguist or translator reviewing your work. Not only will you be making the same mistakes repeatedly, you will be receiving reinforcement that what you are translating is accurate because the errors are not being corrected. Do not confuse silence with approval and acceptance. Many, if not most, clients cannot judge translation quality. This is why the dictum, "I've never had a complaint from a client" is a terrible defense of one's qualifications. The same could be said of coroners or veterinarians, and for the same reason: Your clients are often not in the position to judge quality. All the effort you are putting into humility and learning is lost. In premium markets, you work in collaboration with others, meaning one or more equally-skilled colleagues review every word you translate. Try to imagine that everything you translate goes up on a board at an ATA workshop for everyone to see. That level of commitment to your text, and your solicitation of feedback from everybody in the room, is required to perform at a level that will be necessary as the market shakes out and consolidates to retain the most dedicated translators in the near future.

PERSEVERANCE

Perseverance is committing to humility and collaboration, and then translating, revising and reviewing demanding texts every day. If you just throw your hands up the first time somebody rejects, revises, edits or otherwise questions your translation, you are not going to go very far. Kevin spent well over a decade being revised – meaning heavily edited – on several million words in physics and electronics for publication in the professional science journals before he translated his first physics book. Embrace revision, cooperation, and the wisdom of the crowd. After all, that's how language itself evolves.

Most top-notch clients come to us either through referrals from other translators, or from companies or other direct-client users of our services. In order to be in a position where people refer projects to you, it's necessary to engage directly with your clients. You need to be attending their legal, financial or technical sessions at their conferences (not translation conferences); you need to be in their LinkedIn groups, and you must intellectually and socially inhabit their world. Do not sit at home in isolation with your dictionaries, and spend all your valuable time on social media (which is admittedly still quite useful and valuable as well as socially important).

Social media is incredibly important as one means of "light" collaboration to learn best practices and find answers to your questions (it's no substitute for full-text revision, though); but that alone is not going to sell your services. The degree to which you live in the world in which your clients operate is the measure of success you will have in marketing to them. You want to put yourself in the middle of their world, and not necessarily as a translator. Translators attend conferences and make the grave error of introducing themselves as a translator, which is the worst mistake ¬– as soon as you say the word "translator," you can actually see your potential clients' eyes glaze over as they scan the room for somebody to talk to who knows their industry. The person who knows their industry should be YOU!

Instead, try saying this: "I am Tess Whitty, and I can help you triple your sales in Sweden." Now you have their attention. They do not care what you are, they just want to know how you can triple their sales in Sweden.

What they care about now is how you will accomplish this. So tell them. Then, start talking about their products and services in a way that shows you have intimate knowledge of their products, technology and industry. Now the conversation has become about them. It is about their needs and what they do, how they operate, and what they need. The more you show an interest in a client and their business success, the more that client is likely to trust you. This also reflects the subject-area expertise you need to succeed in producing top-notch translations for this new client. Every psychology study ever done has shown that people buy from people they **like** and from people they **trust**. The degree to which people like you and trust you will determine how successful you are.

*From an interview with **Kevin Hendzel** [www.kevinhendzel.com], an award-winning translator, linguist, author, media consultant and translation industry expert.*

People enter the translating profession at all stages of their careers. Regardless, it's necessary to plan a learning path. If you join a company at a junior level when you leave university, you would expect to receive training, to progress, to be promoted and eventually (if that is the ambition) to end up as a managing director or CEO. Translators likewise don't want to stay at the same level they were at when they first joined the profession, so they need to find ways to advance their careers. This is why continuing education is especially important for translators. It can help you find out whether you want to head in a certain direction, or which specializations to pursue. And if you have already made your decision about whether you want to do media translations, for example, continuing language courses can help you know what to expect and get your foot in the door.

Having a plan is important. Sit down and think about where you want to be heading professionally in the next few months, maybe the next year or so (some people like to plan even further ahead). Decide what you want to achieve; then, having decided, identify a means to help you achieve your goal. It may be some informal training that you want to do, a webinar series, a course or some background reading, or perhaps doing a more in-depth certificate program.

Whatever it might be, find out the options available. Then, book that webinar or course! Read that book! Put aside the time to fully concentrate on the program while you're there, and make sure you follow up on whatever exercises or assignments you might be given. If you do not fully engage with the training you book, if you do not take advantage of everything the training offers, you will not benefit as fully as you deserve.

Once you have finished the course, review what you have learned, and reflect on where it took you. Did it take you to the next stage in your career? If not, is there further reading with which you can follow up?

This is the point to start building on what you have just done, so that by next year you have a plan to take yourself a little bit further in your career, or possibly in another direction. It is important to be deliberate about what you are doing, instead of just going with whatever happens to come up.

From interview with Lucy Brooks and Maia Figueroa
[www.ecpdwebinars.co.uk], who run eCPD Webinars, a continuing education platform for freelance linguists.

MAINTAINING YOUR SECOND LANGUAGE

In all the hustle and bustle of being entrepreneurs and solopreneurs, we can get involved in the business side of things and forget to nurture our actual language skills. This is risky, because languages truly are living. You really need to make a conscious effort to manage your language skills – they are the product you are selling. Here are a few tips to help you stay on top of your skill:

- You must practice. Find a way to practice your speaking skills, listening skills, reading skills, and writing skills. You need to find ways to keep it interesting. Focus and make a conscious effort to practice.

- Make it fun. Don't try to force yourself to read something boring in your second language. You may think it's good for you, but it's much more helpful to read something about which you are excited and passionate.

- Incorporate music and singing into your language practice. Singing information helps us to retain it.

From interview with Eve Bodeux *[www.bodeuxinternational.com], a French to English translator and the author of the book "How to maintain your second language" [bit.ly/Maintaining2ndLanguage].*

Three areas merit consideration as you make plans to protect your business for the future. The first one is to make sure that all your business assets – by this I mean your skills and finances – are solid and secure. Second, you also need to protect yourself, because you and your health are the most important asset of all. Translators work with their brains and bodies – we have to make sure that those are working well in order to be successful. Thirdly, we need to have a strategy and a plan for the future so we can feel fulfilled and make sure that we remain successful and happy.

HOW DO WE PROTECT OUR BUSINESS ASSETS?

Let's start with finances. When I first started, I went from stay-at-home mom to earning extra income. We weren't dependent on my income and I didn't bother to create a financial plan, or calculate my target income. Now, I have shifted from being just a freelancer to being a business. And I feel much more in control and fulfilled these days. My family is also dependent on my income at this time in order to keep up the lifestyle that we have created.

The first step to protecting your finances is to do a cost analysis and figure out what you need to earn to cover the cost of a minimum income. Also figure out a target income, what to strive for and what you would like to earn.

The second step is to create a buffer of at least three months' wages (preferably six months) so you won't panic and make bad decisions when the jobs are few and far between.

The third step is to take precautions to ensure you will get paid. Research clients before engaging with them, and get all job details and agreements in writing. Then, prioritize invoicing and following up. Finally, whether you are working with direct clients or an agency, be sure to have a contract. Very few of us have our own contract template,

165

but we should for those times when the client doesn't provide one. Some translator associations such as ITI and ATA offer model contracts to use as templates. Protect yourself by reading the contracts that you sign, and by understanding your own terms and conditions when you work with clients.

Another asset to protect is your craft. Our business is based on the craft of translation and linguistics skills. So in order to be a successful and sought-after translator, it's important that you focus on keeping your translation skills up to date and of the highest quality.

These days hardly any translators refrain from using translation tools or CAT tools. Many translation companies expect them. You can become much more productive while still ensuring translation quality if you use them. So invest in a tool, keep it updated and master it.

Another rather new phenomenon for translators is the cloud, and cloud-based storage solutions. Many translators use the cloud for backup storage and many translation companies have their translation tools in the cloud. The cloud is largely beneficial as long as we understand the benefits and risks. To be on the safe side, use a professional cloud service with privacy and encryption functions.

Another trend is machine translation, and it's here to stay. It will not replace flesh and blood translators, but it is something that we need to be aware of and learn about. We can use machine translation to our advantage to become more productive. Again, it's important to learn about machine translation so we can both keep up and protect ourselves.

Finally, social media is another factor to consider as a business asset. We can educate ourselves through social media. We can market our services and network with potential clients and colleagues. However, it is important to remember that whatever gets posted online can be traced. So we should never reveal confidential information or complain about customers or colleagues on these platforms.

HOW DO WE PROTECT AND CULTIVATE OUR MOTIVATION AND BALANCE?

One of the biggest challenges freelance translators face is learning how to efficiently and effectively manage time. If we can't manage our time well, we end up working long hours, often inefficiently, and can easily start becoming burned out and despising our work. We need to proactively manage our time and clients, rather than being at the mercy of a hundred different demands streaming in during a single week. Set aside time for self-care and protect your health. Smart freelancers know that they need to eat right, get enough rest, and balance their work with a social life. We need to move our bodies and exercise, otherwise we may get diseases from just sitting in our chairs in front of the computer all the time. Try to devote regular times to work and regular times for other activities.

Another tip is to have a dedicated workspace. Although we can work from anywhere, that isn't always the best idea. We get more done if we work from an office and have ergonomic keyboards and screens and chairs and so forth. Another thing to bear in mind is to protect our motivation by putting ourselves first. It's all too easy for us to put our community, or a client's needs before our own.

As you build your business, you will find you have moments of awesomeness and the next day you might feel completely unmotivated. Just go with the flow, be flexible, and work steadily towards your goals. Focus on helping people instead of just making money. You will feel better and the money will come anyway. Of course, we need to pay our bills, but if we focus just on money, it can lead us to a mindset of not having enough. You may become ungrateful for what you do have and you won't see the freedom and income you are creating because you need more... more... more.... These days my money motivation comes from a place of trying to be grateful for what I do have and helping others, instead of having a negative mindset.

Having a successful mindset means adopting a positive attitude towards everything – including challenges. When things go wrong, you can respond calmly and confidently instead of panicking or playing the victim. So stop complaining about everyone and everything from low rates to bad clients to weird colleagues, and start focusing on how you can develop your business. Make a point of expanding your network and seek out positive, proactive people who inspire you. If you want to create a successful business, mix with like-minded entrepreneurs. Then it's easier to feel more positive. If you feel that you don't have positive, successful people around you, look for them online. Many forums, websites, podcasts and blogs are populated by people who are successful and positive.

HAVING A WORKING STRATEGY FOR YOUR BUSINESS

Don't depend on just one aspect of your business to support complete success, no matter how popular it is. It may work in the short term, but it will fail eventually. Old strategies may fail to engage new customers. Every few years, a new platform emerges that you will find helpful. So don't overlook potential. Don't be afraid to try something new. Part of a good strategy is having vision. Many small businesses lack a clear vision, so they jump from task to task without a clear understanding of what binds individual actions together, or what value they create by their actions. Your vision should provide a cornerstone for everything you do in your business. Is it moving from part-time to full-time translation work, getting better clients and higher pay, or is it becoming known for your expertise? Perhaps you want to add or change specializations, or add additional services, or maybe you want to diversify. The vision you develop can be leveraged into more specific goals. Make sure that your goals are smart goals – specific, measurable, achievable, relevant and time-based.

Here are some questions to ask for creating smart goals:

- What worked last year and what didn't work?
- What will you do next year? Or, in the next six months?

- Where will you market your services? And what methods will you use? Don't create a marketing plan because you feel you have to and then leave it hidden on your computer, or in a drawer. I want you to create a plan for your future, to know where you're going and how you will get there.

Have some simple tactics to use so you don't have to wonder about what to do next, or how you will fit everything into your tight schedule. If you have a plan, it's much easy to take action and follow it. Protect your assets, protect your motivation and balance, and have a vision or a strategy for the future.

From solo episode with Tess Whitty

[www.marketingtipsfortranslators.com/episode-90-protecting-business-ensure-future-success]

CONCLUSION

The Marketing Tips for Translators has become the go-to podcast for freelance translators who want to grow their business and improve their marketing. I personally enjoy listening to podcasts and consuming audiobooks while multitasking, but I am aware that freelancers, and in particular translators, live in a written world. I wanted to make some of the gems from the first 100 podcast episodes available in written format too, and I hope you have enjoyed reading them. Now go out and take some action and grow your business! If you have any questions, feel free to contact me at tess@marketingtipsfortranslators.com. If you want more tips or strategies, you can check out the resources mentioned in the next chapter.

CHAPTER 7 – CONTRIBUTORS

LIST OF CONTRIBUTORS TO THIS BOOK

Corinne McKay [www.thoughtsontranslation.com]

Luca Lampariello [www.thepolyglotdream.com]

Karen Tkaczyk [www.mcmillantranslation.com]

Marta Stelmaszak [www.wantwords.co.uk/martastelmaszak]

Irene Elmerot [www.translationcorner.se/team/irene-elmerot]

Gwenydd Jones [www.translatorstudio.co.uk]

Ted Wozniak [www.tedwozniak.net]

Anne de Freyman [www.adf-translate.co.uk]

Alina Cincan [www.inboxtranslation.com/about/alina-cincan]

Andrew Morris [www.andrewmorris.fr]

Alessandra Martelli [www.mtmtranslations.com]

C.J. Hayden [www.getclientsnow.com]

Sara Freitas [www.sfmtraduction.com/en/sara-freitas]

John Di Rico [www.johndirico.com]

Luke Spear [www.lukespear.co.uk]

Joy Mo [www.proz.com/profile/1180658]

Konstantin Kisin [www.proz.com/translator/82508]

Paul Urwin [www.100percentlanguages.com]

Valeria Aliperta [www.rainylondontranslations.com]

Sara Colombo [www.balanceyourwords.com]

Joanne Archambault [www.traduction-ortho.com]

Ed Gandia [www.b2blauncher.com]

Lisa Carter [www.intralingo.com]

David Rumsey [www.northcountrytranslation.com]

Stever Robbins [www.steverrobbins.com]

Dorothee Racette [www.takebackmyday.com]

Brooks Duncan [www.documentsnap.com]

Karen Rueckert [www.legal-translations-rueckert.com]

Anne Diamantidis [www.marketingtipsfortranslators.com/episode-32-latest-seo-tips-translator-websites-interview-anne-diamantidis]

Catherine Christaki [www.linguagreca.com]

Sebastian Hasselbeck [www.sebastian-haselbeck.de]

Kevin Hendzel [www.kevinghendzel.com]

Lucy Brooks [www.ecpdwebinars.co.uk]

Maia Figueroa [www.ecpdwebinars.co.uk]

Eve Bodeux [www.bodeuxinternational.com]

The Marketing Cookbook for Translators – For a Successful Freelance Career and Lifestyle – Tess Whitty – available on Amazon	
Quick Start Guide: 8 Steps to a Marketing Plan for your Freelance Translation Business – Tess Whitty www.marketingtipsfortranslators.com/resources-2/marketing-plan/	
Quick Start Guide – 10 steps to an optimized website – Tess Whitty www.marketingtipsfortranslators.com/resources-2/quick-start-guide-10-steps-to-optimized-website-for-your-freelance-business/	

How to Succeed as a Freelance Translator – Corinne McKay – available on Amazon	
The Book of Standing Out: Travels through the Inner World of Freelance Translation – Andrew Morris – available on Amazon	
Get Clients Now! (TM): A 28-Day Marketing Program for Professionals, Consultants, and Coaches – C.J. Hayden – available on Amazon	

Warm Email Prospecting: How to Use Short and Simple Emails to Land Better Freelance Writing Clients – Ed Gandia – available on Amazon	
Maintaining Your Second Language: practical and productive strategies for translators, teachers, interpreters and other language lovers – Eve Bodeux – available on Amazon	
Get-It-Done Guy's 9 Steps to Work Less and Do More (Quick & Dirty Tips) – Stever Robbins - available on Amazon	

Made in the USA
Middletown, DE
11 August 2019